LIGHTS FOR THE PATH

If it can't be happy, make it beautiful. Madeleine Davies offers us this exquisite gift, born from her own grief, her compassionate heart, and her listening soul. With elegant simplicity she attends to the fear, fury and fragility of loss, bringing forth wisdom, gentleness and insight in equal measure. Above all she gives us humility and patience, as she lets people tell their own stories and leaves unresolved what no comfort can easily heal. Anyone who faces the agony of loss could wish for no finer companion.

The Revd Dr Samuel Wells, Vicar of St Martin-in-the-Fields, London

This book is quite brilliant. Drawing deeply on the lived experience of the author and her many conversation partners, it offers a beautifully written, keenly observed, and pastorally sensitive resource for making sense of death and bereavement. It is full of practical and psychological wisdom, at once acknowledging the uncertainty and provisionality of life but grounded in a sure faith in the God who does not let us go.

The Revd Canon Dr Joanna Collicutt, Karl Jaspers Lecturer in Psychology of Religion and Spirituality, Ripon College Cuddeson

The stories and personal reflections in this book are indeed 'Lights for the path' of anyone who walks through grief, especially the young, and for those who accompany them. Madeleine Davies' writing is open, accessible, honest and helpful, asking just those questions that so many bereaved people hesitate to put into words. We are going to need good books on grief, like this one, more than ever in the coming days.

The Revd Dr Malcolm Guite, Chaplain, Girton College, Cambridge University

This engaging and easy to read book feels like a hand to hold through the darkest moments of your life. *Lights for the Path* is part memoir and part theological reflection on the theme of death. Skilfully woven together and littered with literary references, Davies offers a gracious acknowledgement and comfort for the whole range of emotions a young person experiencing a death will encounter. Sharing her own story of losing her mum as a teenager, and the stories of others, this book is a window into the deeper questions of life: what happens when we die? Why would God allow this? Davies gives no trite answers; this honest account exposes the simplistic answers for what they are, and creates a safe space to air your true thoughts, your true feelings and your true questions for God. At a time when you might feel most alone, Lights for the Path brings you into a fellowship of brothers and sisters. Although no one would choose to belong to this group, it is a reminder that others have walked a similar path, and that what you are feeling - whatever you are feeling - is perfectly 'normal' and ok. This book is ideal for any teenagers who have lost a loved one, helping them to navigate the grief they are feeling and make sense of faith in the midst of their suffering.

Dr Phoebe Hill, Head of Theology at Youthscape

LIGHTS FOR THE PATH

A Guide through Grief, Pain and Loss

Madeleine Davies

First published in Great Britain in 2020

Society for Promoting Christian Knowledge
36 Causton Street
London SW1P 4ST
www.spck.org.uk

British Library Cataloguing-in-Publication Data
A catalogue record for this book is available from the British Library

ISBN 978–0–281–08356–5
eBook ISBN 978–0–281–08357–2

1 3 5 7 9 10 8 6 4 2

Typeset by Nord Compo
First printed in Great Britain by Jellyfish Print Solutions

eBook by Nord Compo

Produced on paper from sustainable forests

To

my parents, Andy and Alison,
and their grandson, born this springtime

Contents

Acknowledgements

This book emerged after a conversation at The Old Deanery, next to St Paul's Cathedral, with Caroline Chartres, my *Church Times* colleague, who asked me if I had ever thought of writing something a bit longer than newspaper articles. I had, but this chat was the encouragement I needed to get started. I knew immediately that I wanted to include lots of other people's stories, and I am so grateful to all those whose words appear in this book. Those conversations – looking out over the Suffolk marshes with Meryl, in a sunny British Library courtyard with Carrie – are the heart of this book and I'm aware that they come at a cost. My Dictaphone carries proof that on several occasions it was me, not my interviewee apologising for crying. Thank you to Grace for the lasagne and Joanna for the tissues. I want to say a particular thank you to Molly, my youngest interviewee, who was so generous with her story, despite having so recently lost her sister, Dom. I'm also indebted to those who sat down with me to grapple with questions to which there are no easy answers. I'm still drawing on their wisdom in my own life as I continue to try to trust in God's love and power.

Thank you to Elizabeth Neep, my editor, who has always been so enthusiastic about this book, offering not only encouragement and understanding, but her own prayers.

Finally, my family. After my Mum died, I was blessed to have a Dad so full of love, understanding, and faith. I have always been able to tell him anything and this is one of the greatest gifts a parent can offer. Thank you, too, Dad for reading my manuscript so carefully and offering so many encouraging notes in the margins. I'm also blessed with lovely Auntie Liz, Nan, two excellent siblings – Sophie and John – and now a husband, Simon, who is being as supportive as ever by holding our little boy, born just a week ago,

Acknowledgements

as I sit down to write this. I know my Mum would have been the most wonderful grandmother and I look forward to the day when we are all together again.

CHAPTER 1
YOU ARE NOT ALONE

I want my mom back. I want her to knock at my bedroom door
and come walking in. . . I want her all in one piece,
together, with Dad and I again.

Pam in *Alone at Ninety Foot,*
by Katherine Holubitsky

I think I was nine when I first realized that people could die. I was reading a book called *Anne of Green Gables*, the story of a red-haired girl, Anne Shirley, who is adopted by Matthew and Marilla Cuthbert, a brother and sister living in a small town in Canada. It's a book about growing up – intense friendships, fights in the class-room, an extreme hair-dyeing incident – but, like a lot of books written around the early 20th century it includes an early encounter with death. When Anne is 16, Matthew dies, suddenly. When I reached this chapter, I got out of bed and raced across the landing into my parents' room. I wanted reassurance that this wasn't going to happen to either of them.

A year later, when my mum sat my younger sister and me down to tell us that she had cancer, it felt surreal. My little brother was just three. The thing that I was most afraid of was happening, almost as if I had conjured it up. For the next two years, this illness hung heavily over our lives. It set me apart from other people my age. There were hospital visits, tests and worse still, the knowledge that my mum might leave us. What I remember most is a feeling of nausea deep in the pit of my stomach.

Another dimension of this time was my family's Christian faith. Cards with encouraging Bible verses appeared on the mantelpiece

1

above the gas fire, and I clung to the words of a woman who had said she had a feeling that my mum would be healed.

Two years after my mum told us about the cancer, when I was nearly 12, my dad told me that she was going to die. Although I think I knew that this was coming, it still felt unbearable. Over the next few days the house was filled with relatives, friends and nurses. That was in the Autumn, and by Christmas, my beautiful, kind, loving mum was gone.

In one sense, this feels like a very long time ago. More than 20 years have passed, in which time I've finished school, gone to university and unpacked boxes of books and cooking pans in five different flats (and ignored five different landlords' instructions not to use blue tack on the walls). I've managed to get a job as a journalist, overcome my fear of travelling abroad and learned to drive. I'm now the same age as my mum was when I was born, and I'm writing this in the garden of the same house I grew up in, while my husband sits nearby, tapping away at his laptop. I've passed many of the milestones I know my mum wanted to be around for – like buying my first bra and walking down the aisle on my wedding day.

And yet my memories of my mum, and of her death, remain so vivid. I think about her every day, and I still divide my life into two halves: before and after the day she told us she had cancer.

One of the things I remember about those first years without her is how alone I felt. Aged 12, I think I was the only person in my year at school who had lost their mum. When I went back to school, quite soon after the funeral, I remember one girl being surprised and asking, 'Are you over it, then?' I knew then that (a) people, often nice ones, don't always say the right thing, and (b) the way you cope with death may surprise people. I wasn't popular at school, but being 'the girl whose mum died' did mean that people knew who I was.

There were many times in the years that followed when I would be reminded that people don't expect a young person to have lost a parent, like when people asked what my mum did for a job or if she would be picking me up. In fact, I became the person doing the picking up. I took huge pride in trying to fill in for my mum, collecting my younger brother from friends' houses and learning to make a succession of rather basic meals for us for dinner.

Within this busy schedule, I thanked God for books, where I could meet people whose lives looked a bit like mine. Over the years, I found it so comforting to discover that fiction is full of young people who have lost someone – from the Carr girls in *What Katy Did*, growing up without a mother, to Holden Caulfield, the teenage hero of *The Catcher in the Rye*, struggling to deal with the loss of the brother he adores. The author of the Harry Potter books, J. K. Rowling, whose mother died at a young age of multiple sclerosis, once said her books were 'largely about death'. (Daily Telegraph, 2006)[1]

> They open with the death of Harry's parents. There is Voldemort's obsession with conquering death and his quest for immortality at any price: the goal of anyone with magic. I so understand why Voldemort wants to conquer death. We're all frightened of it.

Many fairy tales also feature the loss of a parent; it's striking how many Disney heroes and heroines are affected by it. I was well into adulthood before *Finding Nemo* came out, but I identified a lot with Marlin, the anxious dad who tries to protect Nemo from danger. It was how I felt about my brother and sister.

Books let us know that we are not alone. I decided to write this one because I wanted to recreate the reassuring feeling I got when I

---

1 Geordie Greig, 'There would be so much to tell her' *The Telegraph* (Jan. 2006), <https://www.telegraph.co.uk/news/uknews/1507438/There-would-be-so-much-to-tell-her....html>

came across people who knew what it was like to lose someone they loved. I've called it *Lights for the Path* because I know that life after a death can feel very dark, and I hope that this book might offer a bit of illumination along the way.

Although I don't think that you ever 'get over' the death of someone you love, I do think that, over time, you learn things. One of the most important things I discovered, for example, is that it's possible to carry on loving that person enormously while also moving forward. But for a long time, I felt stuck. I didn't want to get on with my life because it felt like I would be leaving my mum behind. I wondered if this was unusual – had others felt this tension between the desire to remember and an awareness of the need to keep going? Naomi, one of the people I interviewed for this book, told me that after her father died, she found herself 'grasping to find people who had walked this road before me to let me know I would survive'. So, I decided to ask other people who had been bereaved as teenagers about what they had learned along the way, and what advice they might pass on – what lights they might offer you. I've tried to collect a big range of stories because I know that there are many different reasons why you might be reading this book.

In your life, it might not be a parent who is dying or who has died. It could be a brother, sister or friend. For a lot of people, the first person they lose is a grandparent, and that can cause intense pain, especially if they were particularly close to you. If you're worried that your situation means that you don't qualify for this book, please put that thought away – this book is for any teenager dealing with loss (and I hope it might help some older people, too). The person you lost could be a teacher or someone you knew when you were small. As one wise man I interviewed put it: 'If there's somebody who's been a really key part of your life [but] who's not there anymore, it's like losing part of yourself.'

Although you might not think you know anyone who has been bereaved as a teenager, it's not as unusual as you might think. One charity, Child Bereavement Network, estimates that every day, 112 children lose a parent. The number is even higher – one in every 29 children – if you include people who have lost a sibling, and one survey[2] of secondary school pupils found that three quarters had experienced the loss of either a close relative or close friend.

Alongside the real-life stories of the people I've interviewed, you'll find in the chapters that follow an exploration of some of the questions that death can raise: What is death? Is it normal to be so afraid of it? What happens to us after we die? These are questions that humans have thought about, worried about and argued over for thousands of years. When someone dies, these questions are no longer just interesting philosophical topics of discussion – they are about the person you've lost, and where you believe they might be now.

These might seem like strange questions to you. Not everybody believes in Christianity, or even God. Perhaps you've never thought about them before. It could be that you did believe in God, but that losing someone has caused you to become angry at God or maybe reject God altogether. It's also very normal to feel resentful towards people who talk about God when you are grieving. As a teenager, I often got frustrated by people who, after my mum died, said things like 'God will bring good out of this situation.' There's a reason why one of my favourite fridge magnets says 'Please, Jesus, protect me from your followers.' Yet my faith in God has always given me a reason to feel hopeful. I don't believe that death is the end. I do believe that I will see my mum again. In this book, I'll try to explain how I arrived at this belief and introduce you to people who have helped me to understand it.

---

2 Harrison L., Harrison R. 'Adolescent's beareavement experiences. Prevalence, association with depressive symptoms, and use of services.' (Apr. 2001), <https://www.ncbi.nlm.nih.gov/pubmed/11437477>

However much of this book you read, I hope that you'll find at least one light to take with you on your way – whether it's a piece of advice or a story from someone who knows what it's like to be a grieving teenager. It was my mum who gave me my love of books – our house is full of the stories she left for us – and this one is dedicated to her.

CHAPTER 2
HEARING BAD NEWS
(& MERYL'S STORY)

And he knew it was here. He knew there really was no going back.
That it was going to happen, whatever he wanted,
whatever he felt.
Conor in *A Monster Calls* by Patrick Ness

I first learned that my mum had cancer when she took my younger sister and me into our front room, closed the door and began, 'I need to tell you something.' I can vividly remember bolting for the door and her crying after me to come back, as she tried to tell us something about the treatments she was going to have. Life would never be the same again.

Many years later, my dad told me that the prognosis had never been good. By the time it was discovered, the cancer had already spread from my mum's breast to another part of her body. The doctors hoped that treatment would give her more time with us, not cure her completely.

But it was only towards the end of my mum's life that I was certain that she was going to die. My memories of the two years up to my 12th birthday – the week before she died – are all coloured by that diagnosis. I was on the cusp of puberty and frightened of going through it without her. She was afraid, too. 'I don't want to go,' she told us, as we drove up to the hospital where she would be undergoing surgery.

She was still my mum, enormously protective and devoted to us, but I grew up quickly with this threat hanging over us. At home, we put up heartening Bible verses and this famous saying from Julian of Norwich, a medieval nun: 'All shall be well, and all shall be well, and all manner of thing shall be well.' It was not a promise that my mum wouldn't die of cancer, but it was very tempting to read it that way.

A Different Light

Sometimes people who fall in love describe seeing the world in a different light – one full of bright colours and beauty. I think that learning that someone you love is going to die, or has died, can be a topsy-turvy version of this – the world seems to shift on its axis and everything looks dark. Ordinary things seem trivial or even pointless. You're suddenly aware of how fragile life is, and you can scarcely believe that you once felt invincible. It's also possible to feel very powerless. Something that you desperately want to be untrue is happening without remorse.

In the weeks after my mum's diagnosis, it took me a few seconds after waking up each morning to remember what was happening. I hated that daily routine. It was like being shaken awake by the after-shocks of an earthquake. And they would occur during the day as well, sometimes. It's not possible to spend every hour thinking about something so enormous, yet it can still feel surprising that you have managed to do anything else.

Nothing visible marked me out as the daughter of a dying woman, yet I felt transported to an alternative universe in which something profound was occurring to me, and to us, so much earlier than any of us had expected. My godmother gave me a book entitled *The Huge Bag of Worries*, showing a child dragging an enormous blue sack around. My sack was very heavy.

I don't know how much of this may seem familiar to you. Everyone's experience of death is different. That means that there is no 'right' way to deal with it. But in case they are helpful, the things that helped me the most after hearing my mum's diagnosis were:

1. Knowing my teachers understood what was happening
There are many reasons why it can be tempting to keep what is happening in your family private. Telling others can make everything feel more real when you're struggling to face it. Feeling different from others may be the last thing that you want. And people might say the wrong thing. But for me, having teachers who were aware of what was happening meant that, if I struggled in the classroom, they understood why. As it happened, I never needed to leave the classroom, but just knowing that they would have understood, if I'd needed to, lowered my anxiety.

2. Talking to people I trusted
You've probably been warned about the dangers of 'bottling up' emotions. That doesn't mean that you have to tell everyone, or even most people, about what is happening in your life or how it's making you feel. You do not need to feel guilty about being careful about which friends you confide in – you don't 'owe' your story to anyone. But I found that just saying out loud my fears and worries to a few trusted people was a relief, even if nothing they said could take away the cause.

3. Writing things down
I found writing helpful, even just making little notes – I would record a thought or a whole list of anxieties. It was another way of releasing some of the fear taking up space in my mind. Sometimes these would make me cringe; they sounded so dramatic. But I carried on.

I recently found some of these notes, and all I felt was sympathy for the frightened teenage girl who wrote them down. Don't imagine a stranger finding them and judging them – they are just for you.

4. Getting lost in an activity
Even if only a few people know what is happening in your family, you may feel worried that your reaction is being watched or judged. How

can she be playing hockey or laughing over lunch when her sister's dying? On the other hand, the idea that 'life goes on', that you must carry on as normal, can feel brutal. For me, throwing myself into schoolwork helped me to cope. I simply couldn't think about cancer all the time – it was too much. Your escape could be watching films, painting, playing sport or getting lost in a game – being distracted by an activity can be a very healthy way to manage the darkness of grief. We all need space to breathe.

5. Talking to God

If there was one thing that made me feel less alone during this time, it was the belief that God was real and that I could talk to him. I was afraid, but I believed that God was with us, that he cared, that he was good. At times, this was a complicated relationship – I wondered if God would heal my mum and what it meant that 'all shall be well', but I never felt entirely alone. In Psalms we read that God bends down to listen to us. 'My heart has heard you say, "Come and talk with me." And my heart responds, "Lord, I am coming."' Throughout this awful time, that call meant a lot to me.

You might also find that you want time to be alone; that's okay. As a teenager I was lucky enough to have my own room, but for others, this space to think may be found somewhere else like a local library, church or cathedral (many are open during the day), a park, or by asking a teacher at school if there is a quiet room you can go to to be alone for a while.

Kept in the Dark

Although I did not have all the information, I was never kept in the dark about my mum's illness. This isn't everyone's experience. In the past, it was more common to try to 'protect' young people from the reality of terminal illness. In a series of novels about the Cazalet family, author Elizabeth Jane Howard tells the story of Polly, a young woman whose mother dies of cancer. Despite efforts to keep her in the dark, she learns that her mother is ill from her aunt, who lets the information slip, leaving Polly feeling both anxious and angry: 'Fear, like a splinter of ice, had pierced her and she dissolved it in a surge of white-hot, silent rage.'

Information is important because it helps us to prepare for what's going to happen. Without it, you can be left feeling angry when death happens, and lose trust in those who could have shared what they knew. If you feel that you've been left out of important conversations, you might want to seek out information now. The truth can be less frightening than you imagine – there is something particularly scary about whispers, secrets, and mysteries. You might also want to try to learn why you weren't told everything. Often, people think that they are doing the right thing at the time. They may have wanted to protect you or hoped that the person would recover. Talking is an opportunity to understand and to see how, sometimes, people's mistakes were made in love.

'Facing reality' is not something we necessarily want to do. It can make you feel a bit like a detective, trying to dig out a story that you don't even want to uncover. With so many medical treatments available today, it's also sometimes difficult to get definite answers to questions about life and death. It's particularly difficult when people around us may be emphasizing how important it is to have a positive attitude, to believe that someone will get better. Starting to consider the possibility that they might not can feel like giving up, like betrayal. In *A Monster Calls*, a novel by Patrick Ness, Conor, whose mum is very ill with cancer, tries to shut down conversations that feature the words 'after' and 'when this is all over'. Much of the book is about how difficult it can be to confront the truth, but also how necessary: only when Conor shares what he's really afraid of do things begin to get better.

Long Years

My mum was ill for two years before she died. Many young people spend much longer living with a relative with an incurable disease. Death is inevitable, and yet distant. There may be many occasions when it seems close, before retreating again.

Hundreds of thousands of people in the UK are 'young carers', which means that they are providing care for someone who is physically or mentally ill, disabled, or misusing drugs or alcohol. Many aren't receiving any support at all – partly because the truth about their lives is invisible to those outside the home.

In *On Eagles' Wings*, a novel by Sue Mayfield, Tony cannot remember a time when his mum, who has multiple sclerosis, wasn't ill. By the time he's a teenager, he's an expert in helping to care for her, and his feelings oscillate between envy and guilt. He's never had 'the sort of mum who held you tight and made you feel better, who rushed to your bedside to grip your hand and stroke your hair . . . He resented the hours he'd spent looking after her, hated the clinging smell of illness, the tear-stained eyes accusing him.' When his mum goes into hospital, he only learns that she is likely to die when he overhears his father on the phone, describing it as a 'great blessing' – language that makes Tony furious. Does his dad actually want her to die?

Losing a person after a long illness can create confusing feelings. You might have already started mourning for them years earlier, only for them to get better again. Which emergency will prove to be the final one? When the end finally comes, you might feel relief, especially if the person was in pain, and that might, in turn, leave you feeling guilty.

In an episode of the *Griefcast* podcast, the comedian Charlie Russell tells the story of her mother, who died on Charlie's 18th birthday after many years of struggling with bipolar disorder and alcohol abuse. Charlie talks about her memories of trying to look after her mother, even as a young child, and living a 'double life' at home and at school. On the day that her mother died in hospital, she went to her school leavers' ball, where she had an 'amazing time', spending a brief period in a parallel universe in which her mother had never been ill. 'If someone gave me a button that said, "If you press this button your mum hasn't died and it's all different," I don't think I would press it because I was exhausted,' she explained. 'I didn't want my mum to die . . . and I miss her so much, but I also couldn't continue like that anymore. It had been all my life: 18 years of hiding and dealing with my mum not really being a mum. If I could have my mum back, well, I would, but if she were to come back and it were to be like that again, I actually can't do that again.' Charlie felt like a 'fraud' because of these complex feelings of relief, guilt and sadness, and worried, then, that she wasn't 'allowed' to be in the 'club' of people grieving. If you, too, have experienced relief, it's important to know that that's normal and no reflection on your love for the person.

The Horizon

Something else Charlie said during the episode was that she felt that she'd been mourning the loss of her mother since she was 12 years old. If the person you're caring for has an illness that means they are likely to die, even if it's many years in the future, this is a very natural feeling – you may be grieving, while they are still alive, the loss of certain aspects of the person or your relationship with them, and the future that you wish you could enjoy with them. Even happy or special moments can become tinged with sadness as you 'fast forward' in your mind, imagining looking back on these occasions when the person is no longer around. This is known as *anticipatory grief*, Dr John Wyatt, a medical expert and author of a book called *Dying Well*, told me:

> The danger is, if you spend too much time anticipating what is going to happen in the future, you are not actually living in the present. The most important thing is to be there for the person

here and now, rather than spending the whole time thinking about what's going to happen when they die.

His words reminded me of a brilliant woman called Kate Bowler, an American university professor who, at the age of 35, discovered that she had terminal bowel cancer and wrote a book about it called *Everything Happens for a Reason: And Other Lies I've Loved*. One of her pieces of advice, which she learned from a friend, is 'Don't skip to the end.' It made me think of my own habit of flicking to the final pages of books – I like to check that the ending is going to be happy – and how impossible this is in real life. Only God knows what the future holds. 'Living in the moment' can sound a bit cheesy, but it's something that Jesus encouraged us to do, thousands of years ago: 'Do not worry about tomorrow, for tomorrow will worry about itself. Each day has enough trouble of its own (Matthew 6.34).' Knowing the exact date of my mum's death wouldn't have made the two years in which she was ill any easier – I would have just counted down the days anxiously, fixing my eyes on the end.

God's Promise

As you read the stories that end each of the chapters in this book, you'll see that for each person the day they heard that someone they loved was going to die, or had died, has remained a vivid memory. I remember feeling powerless – there was no way I could prevent what was happening to my family. In the next chapter we will look at the impact of a sudden death and the threat this poses to our sense of security. Before we do so, I want to end this chapter with a Bible verse that has become a favourite of mine: 'He won't brush aside the bruised and the hurt and he won't disregard the small and insignificant (Isaiah 42.3, MSG).' It's an Old Testament verse that looks forward to Jesus and what he's like. For me, it's a reminder that when we feel vulnerable, afraid of all the potential harms in the world, like a light that barely has the energy to keep shining, God is especially gentle towards us. God sees our bruises, even if others don't, and doesn't ask anything of us at this time. He doesn't promise us that bad news will never come to our door, but he does promise to be with us, always.

Meryl's Story

When I was a small child, one of my favourite books was called *The Very Worried Sparrow*. This sparrow is anxious about lots of things: what he's going to eat, how to build a nest. Even as a child, I identified a lot with this little bird. But it wasn't until about 30 years later, when I got a job as a journalist, that I discovered that the author, Meryl Doney, was married to one of my colleagues, Malcolm. One day Malcolm talked about how much he wished he had met Meryl's dad, who died when she was 17. When I told him about this book, he suggested that Meryl and I meet and so, one sunny spring afternoon, I travelled to their beautiful house in the Suffolk countryside.

I immediately got a sense of how much Meryl loved her dad. 'He was one of those people who is interested in everything,' she told me. 'He used to make things, he used to paint, and we used to build things together. I was the right-hand person, really. He was almost my best friend.' Meryl's dad had always had problems with his stomach, but, although she could see that it was getting more severe, she wasn't told about his diagnosis of stomach cancer. She reflected:

> I regret they didn't take us in to see him after he died because you never quite know that they have gone [if you don't], and you always expect them to come back again though the door. I would have liked to have had more of a conversation, when he got the diagnosis – to have been treated like an adult. And I would have liked to have had more of a conversation about his past and his life.

At the funeral, she found herself 'just imagining his hands, thinking, "In that box are those hands that are really important to me." I used to sit in church with him and hold his hand.' But she also remembers thinking that she needed to be strong, and in the years that followed, she took on quite a lot of responsibility in her family.

> I was the one who could drive, so I took the car and I just felt that that was a moment of growing up really, finally. I didn't do a lot of grieving because I felt I had to keep the show on the road. There was this great big gaping hole where my dad was [had been], and I felt that I had to step into it.

Meryl became a Christian a year or two before her dad died. 'I was rather a certain person and, after he died, I had no doubts that although it was absolutely devastating for us, he was somewhere else in a much better place and that I would see him one day,' she told me. I found it really encouraging to hear that this is something she still believes today:

> When you see somebody who has died, you know that it isn't them; something real has gone, something animating, a real quality is just not there. If you look at how many things we are discovering, just about the ordinary world that we know, it makes all kinds of sense to me that this is by no means all there is, and that personality is so real in people that it will carry on.
>
> After Jesus was resurrected, he had got a body that people could see and react to; it wasn't wafty – people could touch him, he ate things. I don't know what we will look like in heaven, but I think we'll know one another, like you know an essence of somebody even if their look changes. And I am really looking forward to that.

None of this means that Meryl doesn't miss her dad. 'Sometimes, when something really interesting happens, I sort of say, "Hey, how about that Dad!"' she told me.

It would be so nice to share all the things I've done with him. I'd be so interested to know what his reaction would be and talk through things with him. It would be interesting to know how he would have got on with my husband, and what he would have thought of my children. I want to pass him on to the next generation. Although my husband is totally different in many ways, there is something about his spirit which is like my dad's – the funniness, the humour.

Hearing Meryl talk about her dad reminded me that, even after many years have passed, the people we love are still so real to us, that we still think about them and their place in our lives. 'You can say to yourself, "God is still with me, the one who had died is with God and they are still themselves,"' she told me, when I asked what advice she might give to people who have lost someone.

You are allowed to be sad, and sadness will come at odd times, and you just let it come. Tears are good – let them go. And finding somebody to talk to is good. You are you, and the things that you are feeling are fair enough, and you will get through it.

CHAPTER 3
WHEN DEATH IS SUDDEN
(& MOLLY'S STORY)

There was no premonition, no hint of danger round the corner.
Death waited expectantly, hunched in the shadows.
The Lost Boys Appreciation Society
by Alan Gibbons

Grief after a sudden death is different from grieving when we know that someone is going to die. An unexpected death is shocking, which is why, so often, people feel numb or wonder if they are dreaming; it's almost impossible to take in what has happened. It can leave us feeling extremely vulnerable, wondering what else might, with no warning, go wrong. 'Sudden death completely pulls the rug from under your feet,' explained Isobel Bremner, a counsellor who leads the Candle Child Bereavement Service, working with young people at St Christopher's, a hospice in London. 'It completely changes everything . . . It undermines everything you have taken for granted.'

While those who know that someone they love is dying may spend a long time anticipating it, those hit by a sudden death may find their thoughts going over the past to try to identify a warning, or to imagine how life might have turned out differently, if only this or that had been done, or not done. Often, there was no opportunity to say goodbye.

Sudden, violent deaths also need investigation, and people who work in medicine, law, the criminal justice system, and perhaps also the media, will seek to determine exactly what happened.

This can feel like another loss of control, as strangers take charge of the process.

With No Warning

When death is sudden, it often feels surreal. We are so used to watching tragic scenes on our screens that it can be difficult to absorb the reality that it is really happening, and to you. Eileen, who was 17 years old when her mother died suddenly of a brain haemorrhage, remembers how surreal it was to come back from the hospital to a meal her mum had prepared earlier. 'For weeks after, if a knock came on the door, you'd think, "Oh, it's my mam," and you'd jump up, just momentarily, thinking "Oh, she's here,"' she told me.

The sheer speed at which events occur can also leave you spinning. In emergencies, professionals swing into action, to try to preserve life or to cordon off crime scenes, to establish what has occurred. You might have felt that you barely had an opportunity to comprehend what was happening around you. Not knowing the facts can mean that you're left with questions that trouble you: Was there anything else the doctors could have done? Was the person in pain? If you do have questions, write them down – it's never too late to ask a doctor.

Dr John Wyatt believes that understanding what has happened is an important part of the grieving process: that in order for us to process things emotionally, we need to grasp the facts. 'There is a real value in providing detailed medical explanations, even if it feels cruel,' he told me. 'Some people do say that they don't want to know, but interestingly, my experience is that is nearly always the older generation . . . It's actually quite unusual to find an adolescent who says, "I don't want to know."' He always tries to treat teenagers like adults.

He also believes that it's often helpful to see the person who has died. 'The biggest fears are the fears of the unknown,' he explained. 'If you don't actually see the reality, what you are left with is an imagining in your mind of what they look like, and often, the imagined is much worse than the reality.'

A helpful thing to remember is that whatever the person looks like, they are still them. We are more than our bodies. Towards the end of my mum's life, her skin was very yellow and she slept a great deal, almost like a weary baby. It was very difficult to see her like this but she was still my mum, and those memories are just one part of the story that I carry around in my head now. I also remember the fancy leather boots that she splurged on one winter, the petal-skirt she created out of purple silk when I wanted to look like a Flower Fairy, and how fiercely she loved and protected me.

What If . . .

A sudden death can leave you with regrets, wishing you could have said goodbye or sorry or 'I love you.' Or it may leave you repeatedly going over the events shortly before the death and fantasizing about whether, if things had been different, the person would still be alive. What if they had got an earlier train home or someone else had picked them up from the station? It seems incredible that small, trivial events can end a life, and turn yours upside down.

When Cathy Rentzenbrink was 17, her brother, Matty, was knocked down by a car. He never walked or spoke again, and was eventually diagnosed as being in a permanent vegetative state. In her memoir, *The Last Act of Love*, she describes how Matty turned down the offer of a lift home from a club. 'This is the moment,' she writes. 'If I could go back in time and force him to come with me then everything would be different.' She describes how, over the years, she started to doubt her memories of the night. Did she manage to find him to tell him about the lift? Did she stop trying to find him?

Dr Wyatt says that feelings of guilt are very common, not just in cases of sudden death: 'It's often not expressed – it's just a deep, deep anxiety that people find almost impossible to acknowledge, even to themselves, let alone another person.' It's one of the reasons he thinks it's so important to provide detailed information about exactly how a person died, so that he can explain to the person feeling guilty that 'What you did didn't make any difference, or what you didn't do – it would have happened just the same way.'

In his book on supporting children and young people who've experienced trauma, the psychologist Dr Atle Dyregrov writes that guilt is 'often about a lack of perspective about one's own role'. He has found that young adults can be 'extremely judgemental of themselves and of their reactions and impose unreasonable demands with regard to what they should or should not have done'. Part of his work has entailed helping them to recognize that the decisions they took may have been the right ones given the information they had at the time. One of the questions he asks is 'What would you have thought if somebody else had done what you did? Would you have criticized him or her for this?'

Death on the Road

Sudden deaths can take many forms, including accidents, heart attacks or strokes, and violent deaths. If you were not aware of a diagnosis, death after a long, hidden illness can seem sudden.

When my dad's father died in a car accident in the 1950s, around 5000 people a year were killed in this way. Today the number is much lower; cars are safer today and there are strict laws about seatbelts and drink-driving. But it's still the second-biggest cause of death for boys aged 5 to 19. In 2018, there were 1784 road deaths in the UK – an average of five people every day.

Although we talk about car 'accidents', and very few people intend to harm anyone on the roads, these deaths can involve hard questions about guilt and blame. Sometimes families prefer to talk about a 'crash', rather than an 'accident', and to say that the person was 'killed' rather than that they 'died'.

In Britain, after someone dies in a car accident, a family liaison officer (FLO) from the police should get in touch with you. Part of their job is to answer any questions that you might have about the crash. Michelle Ford, an FLO in Lincolnshire, told me that while 'utter disbelief and shock' is common, different family members may react differently: 'Some want every piece of information and some want nothing.'

After someone dies in a crash, there is likely to be a post-mortem: a medical examination of their body to work out the cause of death. If you want to read this report, you have the right to. The doctor who writes it, called a pathologist, may also be able to answer questions that you have about how the person died and what they experienced beforehand. You might also want to go to the scene of the crash to understand what happened, and to leave something as a memorial, such as flowers or a letter.

It's the job of the police to investigate the crash to find out exactly what happened and why. There are various offences that a person can be charged with, but it's important to remember that just because someone is charged with a crime, it doesn't mean they will definitely be found guilty – that is for a court to decide. If you want to find out more, Brake, the road safety charity, has a really detailed guide on their website that you can download for free.[1]

It's up to you as to how much you want to be involved in a case. You may want to attend every court hearing that takes place; some families feel strongly that they want to see the person being prosecuted and learn as much as possible about the case against them. Others may decide that it would be too painful to hear about the crash in detail and to listen to lawyers defend the person accused of helping to cause it. Remember that you can leave a courtroom at any time and that it's natural to feel a mix of emotions. You may feel intense anger towards other people involved in the crash, and you may feel sorry for them, too.

---

1 'Information and advice for bereaved families and friends following death on the road in England and Wales.'

In *The Last Act of Love*, author Cathy Rentzenbrink recalls the day on which a magistrate heard the case of the driver who knocked down her brother, eventually fining him £180. 'I just felt sad,' she writes. 'I felt sorry for the driver and imagined how I'd feel if I'd done something like that to someone.'

For other families, the desire is for the defendant to serve a long sentence. In *The Spying Game*, a novel by Pat Moon, Joe, whose father is killed in a collision, is consumed by the rage he feels towards the other driver. 'It would have been different if it had been a gun or something,' he observes. 'But a car's a weapon, isn't it? If it kills someone?'

When I asked David Radford, a retired judge, about sentences for those charged with death by driving offences, he agreed that bereaved families were often dissatisfied, even though the maximum sentences have been increased over the years. 'Emotionally, it is seen as a murder, but it is not,' he explained. For Judge Radford, it's important to remember that, unlike murder, most deaths by dangerous driving are not deliberate. In some cases, it is a momentary loss of concentration by the driver that causes a death. That driver may feel intense guilt and remorse. Is it always right to send them to prison?

Forgiveness

When someone is killed, thoughts of revenge aren't unusual. In *Living with Grief After Sudden Loss*, Lula M. Redmond, a nurse who set up a support group for survivors of murder, described how people were often ashamed of having rage-filled thoughts of vengeance, and were frightened by them: 'Such retaliatory thinking is quite typical and expected under the circumstances,' she writes. '[But] It is in venting and verbalizing the [their own] murderous impulses that the anger begins to lose some of its intensity and power.' Sometimes, it can help to draw images of these thoughts.

Stephen Cherry, dean of King's College Cambridge, shared with me his concern that, too often, people who have been hurt or harmed are told that they must forgive immediately. We need to think more carefully, he says, about what we are asking of victims, and about the burdens we may be placing on them when we tell them that they must simply forgive. 'It's really bad if the Church isn't able to help people embrace anger, and allow anger to be healthy,' he told me. Yes, we should help them to move away from hatred, but 'anger is an emotion which arises to alert you and others that things are wrong.' The Bible talks about forgiveness and mercy, but it also talks about truth and justice. All of these things matter. Forgiveness is often only possible, he thinks, after the person has accepted that they have done something wrong and expressed remorse. It is a gift, and it's not likely to happen quickly.

This is only one way to think about forgiveness. I have come across wonderful stories of people who have been able to forgive those who have been responsible for the most terrible crimes against their families, even before any repentance has been expressed. Your own forgiveness journey will be unique – it may be different from that of other people in your family – but if you're struggling with forgiveness, please know that you are not alone.

Grieving a Suicide

Miranda was 15 when her brother took his own life at the age of 25. She remembers him as 'Funny, generous and cool. All my friends fancied him. He doted on me . . . I remember him teaching me to tell the time and organizing treasure hunts.' She did have an awareness that something was wrong for a year or two before he died. She remembers overhearing her mother saying that he should see a psychiatrist. She also remembers that she told a school friend that her brother was unhappy, 'And that I didn't know what to do.' But even today, she is still piecing together exactly what happened.

> I remember the day he died very clearly. I saw the police car arrive at our front door, and later, my father, who was distraught,

came up to my room to say that there had been a terrible accident and that my brother had fallen from a building. I waited for him to say that we were going to see him in hospital. When he didn't, I assumed that must mean that my brother was dead. Nobody actually used these words and, again, it was left to me to work out what had happened from the conversation among the adults.

If someone you love has taken their own life, you may feel very alone. But it's not as uncommon as people think. In 2018, there were 6507 suicides in the UK, and the charity, Winston's Wish, estimates that every day, eight people under the age of 16 lose a parent to suicide. They describes these deaths as a 'double blow', because families not only have to deal with a sudden, often unexpected, death, but also the way in which the person died. One person told them that it was like 'grief with the volume turned up'. Feelings of guilt, shame and self-blame can arise, and all the while, there are questions hanging in the air: Why did this happen? Could it have been prevented? How could the person do this to you? Did they mean to die? What weren't they telling me?

Albert Y. Hsu, an American writer, was 25 when his father took his own life after becoming depressed due to a stroke. In his book, *Grieving a Suicide*, Albert writes that hearing about a suicide means being 'plagued by our imaginations . . . Whether we witnessed the death or not, we replay images over and over in our head, like a movie on a loop that we can't turn off.'

Questions may come from outside, too. You might feel that you're the focus of other people's morbid curiosity or judgement. One study found that young people at university who had been bereaved by a suicide were more likely to lie to others about the cause of death.

Alone at Ninety Foot is Katherine Holubitsky's story about 14-year-old Pamela, whose mum has taken her own life by jumping from a bridge. 'You're wondering why she did it,' Pamela tells us, the readers of her story, early on. She describes how the death 'instantly made me into some kind of freak' at school. 'Some kind of fragile being that had to be tip-toed around so I wouldn't shatter at the slightest word . . . I hated being singled out.' Remember that you don't owe anyone the story of what happened. It's okay to say something like 'I'd rather you didn't ask me any more questions.' But know, too, that you have nothing to be ashamed of.

Silence

Miranda remembers that her family became used to 'steering clear of words that caused pain'. There were no photographs of her brother in the house, and her father sometimes tore the opening page out of a book if it had her brother's name written on it 'because it was unbearable even to see his handwriting'.

> I don't blame any of them for this behaviour. We were all in a lot of pain and wanted to rebuild our lives. But, however understandable our responses . . . we robbed ourselves of the chance to talk about someone we had all loved . . . I envied a friend whose brother had also died, but of an illness, and whose family often talked about him and had lots of photos of him in the house. They kept him present, while we seemed to lose my brother all over again, by not acknowledging him. It felt as though there were something 'cleaner' about a death from illness as opposed to a suicide. I think we felt ashamed, guilty, and angry. If only we had been better educated about mental illness and understood that it wasn't our fault, or his, that my brother had become ill. I hope the greater openness with which mental health is discussed nowadays will not only save lives, but help assuage the grief of families bereaved by suicide.

This openness is something that is being championed by Stephen Manderson, a rapper known as Professor Green. In 2015, he created a documentary for the BBC called *Suicide and Me*, in which he explored the suicide of his dad seven years earlier. He made the film in order to get a better understanding of why his dad had done what he did by talking, for the first time, to friends and family about his dad's life. In addition to exploring his troubled relationship with his dad, who was largely absent during his childhood, Stephen also described worrying about his own risk of suicide and passing that tendency on to his own children. But he's reassured by a conversation he has with a psychotherapist who points out:

> We're having a conversation about it [now]; you're confronting the pain about it and that's different. It's a really important difference between you and him. That means you are not condemned, in a sense, to the same path you are worried about.

Talking helps. During the film, Stephen shares that he has been able to sleep for eight hours straight for the first time in a long time.

Why?

Suicide isn't always completely unexpected. It may be that the person has attempted to take their own life before or has threatened to. The Samaritans say that about 90 per cent of people who die by suicide have a mental health problem at the time. Albert Y. Hsu reminds us that it's important to see the difference between a 'cause' and a 'trigger'. Sometimes people, including the media, latch onto a single reason for a person taking their own life, such as a break-up, argument or loss of a job. But the reality is suicide is never the result of a single factor.

It might be that you need to hear this from Winston's Wish: 'It is so important to remember that nothing anyone says or doesn't say, or does or doesn't do, can cause someone to die by suicide. In the same way, you cannot prevent someone from taking their own life.' Reread that as many times as you need to.

Deaths on the road and suicide are, of course, only two forms of sudden death. But I hope that some of the stories in this chapter may have helped you feel less alone with the complex feelings you may be struggling with.

Molly's Story

The first thing I noticed in the Wrights' family home were the beautiful photos on the walls of David, Angela, and their two daughters, Dominique and Molly. 'We've always spoken about Dom, and had pictures,' David told me. 'We've not forgotten about her – she's there.'

Dom was 23 when she died. She was the passenger in a van driven by her boyfriend, Ben, who was over the alcohol limit when he crashed into a tree in the early hours of an October morning in 2016. Even though Molly, who was about to take her mock GCSEs when Dom died, is still trying to process what happened, she very kindly agreed to speak to me in the hope that it might help others. 'I still don't really believe it or understand it,' she told me.

Concentrating in lessons was difficult for Molly when she returned to school, but she worked incredibly hard at breaktimes and at home. 'It made me think about one thing [school], and if I thought about that I didn't have to think about Dom,' she explained. The school arranged for her to take her exams on her own in a room, and to have rest breaks and in the end, she did amazingly well, getting nine 'A' stars. But she felt sad rather than happy when she collected the results: 'I felt like I had ignored what was really going on for such a long time.'

Molly was also often worried about other people's feelings. She felt that it was 'unfair' to talk to friends too much, for fear of upsetting them, and she felt 'really, really protective' of her parents. 'I don't want them to see me hurting because if they see that, it would just break them even more, and I know it works the same for me. When I see them upset, I get a lot more upset.' But she also described the three of them as 'a little team' who had 'got each other through everything'.

I thought her advice to friends was excellent:

Just treat me normally. I don't want to feel like a monster and feel like it's [the grief] a burden all the time, but also, if I want to talk about it or if they want to hear about it, they don't need to say anything. You don't need to have anything to make me feel better.

Since the accident, Molly's family have done a huge amount towards making roads safer. David participated in a short film for the police, telling the family's story to try to deter others from drinking over the limit, and Angela organized a fundraising ball for Brake. Molly, who has also raised lots of funds, has mixed feelings:

I find it nice knowing I am raising a lot of money and raising awareness but I always get quite frustrated that you have to raise a lot of money for something that should be simple, like how to follow the rules and how to be safe.

Ben pleaded guilty to causing Dom's death and was jailed for two years, but rather than being driven by the desire for revenge, the Wrights supported Ben, going every other week to prison to visit him. Molly explained:

It's more out of respect for my sister, really. Because she was in love with him, and none of this was on purpose . . . Dom was a really, really forgiving person and she always wanted to move on and be happy again, and I think if she thought our lives were full of hate and despair and Ben's was as well, I think it would make her feel worse and we just want to just make Dom's memory happy rather than hateful.

[Grief] changes day to day. Most of the time, at the moment, I'm just really, really, sad . . . I just want to be alone, don't want to talk to anyone, just want to feel like everything's really rubbish and there's not really a point . . . And, sometimes I am okay and just try to remember happy things . . . more recently I've just felt really, really angry and frustrated, because I don't have a reason why.

Something that has helped the whole family is hearing about the impact that Dom had in her lifetime and how many people loved her. Dom was a very caring older sister who looked after Molly, and often let her pick out outfits. Today Molly always likes to have a piece of Dom's clothing on her or wear her perfume 'Just to feel like she's with me.' It's about being both similar and different from her sister, she reflects.

It's definitely important not to be a clone . . . That's what upset me at the start, when people would say 'You look like Dom.' I'd think 'But I don't.' I felt like I was just kind of there – just to fill in the gaps because she wasn't here. But obviously, that's not true.

Her advice for others is not to put a time limit on grief: 'If you try to say, "Right, I'll be fine in a year," it just feels worse when you're not. Talk to people. Talk to your parents and talk to your friends because they want to help you.' Before heading to university next year, she is going to take some time out to work in France. It will mean meeting new people and she sometimes worries about how to tell them about what happened three years ago, but she has learned that true friends just want to care for you. I think Dom would be incredibly proud of her.

CHAPTER 4
WHAT IS DEATH?
(& SAM'S STORY)

Bones can snap. Skin is like paper. And I just want to go back.
I want to go back to when it felt like nothing could hurt me.
Lucy 'Bird' Hansson in
The Names They Gave Us by Emery Lord

The idea of death is so enormous that, if we dwell too much on it, it can feel as if it's going to swallow us up. When I woke up one November morning, knowing that my mum was likely to have died during the night, I sat in bed just thinking about the sheer strangeness of it all. Researchers think that until we are about eight years old, we don't fully understand what death is. Young children aren't able to grasp that death is permanent, irreversible and universal – that it happens to everyone and it can't be undone. As we grow up, death may become our greatest fear. It's also something that many of us try to avoid thinking about.

Nothing at All?

For some people, the answer to coping with their fear is to minimize death. A popular poem read at funerals is 'Death Is Nothing at All', by Henry Scott Holland. It begins: 'Death is nothing at all. I have only slipped away to the next room.' A few summers ago, at a festival, I heard another poet, the Revd Malcolm Guite, ranting about this poem. 'Death isn't "nothing at all"! Telling people it is just makes them feel guilty about their sadness,' he said. Malcolm had also discovered that the poem had, in fact, been taken from a sermon by Henry Scott Holland, which said a lot more about death than those few lines. In fact, it described death as a 'disaster'. You can find the whole sermon on Wikipedia. It's called 'The King of Terrors', and I found it a brilliant summary of some of my own fears about death. We are afraid because it's so mysterious, Henry Scott Holland observes. While we are here, alive, we can't possibly experience what happens when we die. But at the same time, we should hold onto our belief that death isn't the end. Even if the idea that those who we love are simply in 'the next room' isn't helpful, God has promised eternal life. Just because we don't yet know all the answers doesn't mean we need be afraid; if we believe that God loves us, we can trust him beyond death.

'Regarding the question . . .'

We know from the Bible that our questions about all of this – what death is, what happens afterwards – aren't new. In a letter in the New Testament, Paul wrote:

> Regarding the question, friends, that has come up about what happens to those already dead and buried, we don't want you in the dark any longer. First off, you must not carry on over them like people who have nothing to look forward to, as if the grave were the last word. Since Jesus died and broke loose from the grave, God will most certainly bring back to life those who died in Jesus. (1 Thessalonians 4:13–14, MSG)

It was the passage that we read at the graveside when we buried my mum, and I've always liked it because it's a reminder that the very first Christians were anxious about death, too. Instead of telling them not to worry, Paul wanted to comfort them. He wrote about having 'complete confidence' in what he was saying because it had been told to him by Jesus himself, and he encouraged people reading his letter to 'reassure one another'.

Despite this message of ultimate hope, Jesus understood grief. When he found people crying at the grave of his friend Lazarus, he didn't tell them off. The Bible tells us that he cried and was 'deeply moved' and 'troubled'. Some translations say that he 'groaned' or even that a 'deep anger welled up within him'. There are lots of different ways in which people have interpreted this verse, but I've always read it as being about Jesus' compassion for the grieving, his longing for the day when death is no more.

Sound of Silence

Despite the fact that death happens to us all, it's something that we rarely talk about. When my mum died, I wasn't aware of anyone else of my age, apart from my sister and brother, who had lost a parent. I felt I was grappling alone with something enormous, that I'd crossed into another part of life earlier than I was supposed to, gaining a sort of wisdom I had never asked for. Matt Fitzgerald, a pastor in America, remembers the anger he felt, aged 15, after his father died. 'I sneered at intact families. I wanted everyone to know what I knew, to suffer something of what I was suffering,' he wrote in *Christian Century* magazine (24 October 2018). 'The people you love are going to die! You are! I am! We . . . croak.'

People often avoid using the word *death* at all. 'Why do we keep saying Mum *went away*?' asks Billy, a teenager whose mum has died, in Mimi Thebo's novel *Wipe Out*. 'She didn't go away. She died. Mum died, Dad. Mum is dead.' When I began writing this book, I became curious about whether this was always the case. How did people in the past think, feel and talk about death?

In her book *Death's Summer Coat*, Dr Brandy Schillace, an American historian, writes about how we have begun to 'fear it [death] as an enemy', whereas generations before us saw death as inevitable. The medical system has joined us in 'the fight against death'. Not long ago it would have been those who grew up *without* losing someone close to them who would have been seen as unusual. The Office for National Statistics tells us that in 1900 life expectancy was around 50 years.

It wasn't that death wasn't strange or mysterious, rather that more people were touched by it earlier. While researching her book *The Fiery Chariot*, historian Lucille Iremonger worked out that two thirds of all of our prime ministers in the 19th and early 20th centuries had lost a parent by the age of 15. Many famous people who achieved great things lost one or even both parents at a very early age. One of the things that connected Paul McCartney and John Lennon of the Beatles was that both of them had lost their mothers as teenagers. The actress Charlize Theron was 15 when her mother shot her father dead in an act of self-defence, while former US President Barack Obama was ten when he saw his father for the last time before his death in a car accident ten years later.

Dr Schillace believes that not talking, or even thinking, about death has caused it to become 'foreign and unfamiliar' and left us unprepared for grief. She suggests that learning about how people in history, and in different cultures, have dealt with it can help us. Grieving is something that unites us all, across time and space. 'In dying – and in knowing that we die – we are among friends, connected in that sense to human culture past and present,' she writes.

Death Yesterday and Today

About a year before I was born, Philippe Ariès, a French writer, published an enormous book called *In the Hour of Our Death*. It tells the story of how people in the West have thought about death over the last 1,000 years – from the time of King Arthur's Knights of the Round Table to the development of the modern hospice movement, which was started at St Christopher's Hospice in South London.

One of the things that this book taught me is that, in the early Middle Ages, death used to be 'tame': it was something familiar to people, something you didn't resist because it was inevitable. Often, it was described as 'sleeping' – a term which some people still use today. You've probably heard people use the phrase 'Rest in peace'.

This doesn't mean that our ancestors didn't experience grief. They loved life, and saw death as a sign of the existence of evil. But they were conscious, too, of the world to come. Today, many people continue to believe in life after death (including me!) But hundreds of years ago, it seems almost everyone did.

Philippe Ariès found that from the 15th to the 19th centuries, the cross was the dominant image in the places where people were buried. For hundreds of years now, people facing death have put their faith in what those two intersecting bars represent. The cross symbolizes not only death, but what happened after Jesus died upon it: resurrection.

Like many throughout history, I have grown up believing that when Jesus died on the cross, he defeated death once and for all. 'Thine be the glory!' we sang at my mum's funeral, with its promise that 'death has lost its sting'. Paul explains this in another New Testament letter, 1 Corinthians, writing:

> If there's no chance of resurrection for a corpse, if God's power stops at the cemetery gates, why do we keep doing things that suggest he's going to clean the place out someday, pulling everyone up on their feet alive? And why do you think I keep risking my neck in this dangerous work? I look death in the face practically every day I live. Do you think I'd do this if I wasn't convinced of your resurrection and mine as guaranteed by the resurrected Messiah Jesus? . . . Not on your life! It's resurrection, resurrection, always resurrection, that undergirds what I do and say, the way I live. (1 Corinthians 15: 29–32, MSG)

Paul lived a life of risk because he was so confident that just as Jesus had come back from the dead, so would he, and all of us, one day.

Death, the Enemy

When I read about Paul's life of adventure, I sometimes wonder if I could ever have his level of confidence. Richard Dawkins, an atheist, once suggested that if Christians really believed in God, they wouldn't be afraid to die.

Yet, for me at least, fear isn't easy to set aside. It's not just the fear of death that we have to deal with, but the thought of leaving those we love behind. This doesn't make us less Christian. After all, God loves the world he created. In the New Testament, death is described as the enemy. The feelings that death can stir up in us – anger, outrage, grief, etc. – are a reminder that death was never part of God's plan for us. God is on our side when we long for the day when death no longer exists.

Dr John Wyatt believes that, ultimately, Jesus has overcome death, but he still describes it in his book, *Dying Well*, as a 'mysterious and dreadful enemy, a threat, a destroyer'. He believes that our instinct to regard death as 'an outrage, an alien interruption into the goodness of reality' is right: it reflects God's original plan for humanity. After all, he writes, 'We were not intended to die; we were made to live forever.'

For Dr Wyatt, medicine's fight against death is a sign to the world of God's ultimate victory over death. Ultimately, only God can destroy death, but the ways in which doctors can cure diseases and save lives are glimmers of that ultimate triumph. In fact, from the earliest days of the Church, Christians have been at the forefront of medicine, caring for the sick and the dying. Dr Wyatt told me that he's noticed that many people who lose someone they love – not just Christians – go on to work as doctors or nurses, or to hold other positions in medicine and other helping professions – joining this struggle.

Freedom Fighters

When I began writing this book, the same verse turned up for three weeks in a row, in three different churches I was visiting. It's a verse about Jesus:

> The Saviour took on flesh and blood in order to rescue them by his death. By embracing death, taking it into himself, he destroyed the Devil's hold on death and freed all who cower through life, scared to death of death. (Hebrews 2:15, MSG)

Some translations speak about freedom for 'those who all their lives were held in slavery by their fear of death'. To be a captive of fear is to feel powerless, held back from living a life of joy and freedom. It's how I felt during the years when my mum was ill, and for years afterwards. I was afraid. This isn't the life that God wants for us.

One of the people I talked to about this is Dr Joanna Collicutt. She is both a priest and a psychologist, and she helps people in the Church to think about death, dying and heaven. One of the interesting things she told me was that Jesus' victory over death was a victory over the *fear* of death, over death's power to stop people being who they were made to be. She got me thinking about all the ways in which a fear of death can hold us back. I know that there have been times when I've wasted many hours worrying about it – time that I could have spent doing the things that I love.

Joanna explained that Jesus taught that there was 'another vision to be had, another story to be told,' a 'cosmic perspective' in which death is not all-powerful. 'This earthly life isn't the end, either in the sense of time or the sense of end, in terms of the goal,' she said.

I like this description – this idea that we can try to live with another story in mind. Another helpful thing she told me was that it's okay to be honest about our fears, to 'own up to the fact that it's frightening as a reality'.

Today, when I think of the offer of being freed from fear, I think of a set of photographs by the artist Sam Taylor-Johnson. By the age of 40, she had been treated for two types of cancer. Shortly after being treated the second time, she made a series of self-portraits – photographs that show her suspended mid-air (the ropes used are invisible), floating above the ground in graceful poses. 'I made them shortly after I was no longer referring to myself as an ill person,' she explained. 'There is a definite sense of physical freedom from the constraints of illness. My biggest fears aren't with my work. My biggest fears are [about] walking through hospital doors. Once you can face that, being fearless about your work is easy.'

Although this wasn't how Sam Taylor-Johnson described them, I look at these photos as a reminder of the freedom Jesus brings, and as a picture of the way that God holds us – not like the ropes that held the artist, but as a loving father who surrounds us with his love while we grow in confidence to live lives unencumbered by fear. Perhaps for those of us who struggle to live in this freedom, the best that we can do is to give our fears to God. There wouldn't be so many verses in the Bible about fear if it wasn't such a common human emotion, if we weren't so desperately in need of comforting, reassuring words.

Mourn with Those Who Mourn

The Bible promises that one day, 'There will be no more death or mourning or crying or pain,' (Revelation 21:4 NIV) but that day hasn't come yet. It also tells us to 'Rejoice with those who rejoice; mourn with those who mourn,' (Romans 12:15 NIV) Mourning is a word that we don't often use today. It describes how we show our sadness after someone dies.

One figure in history that people often turn to when thinking about mourning is Queen Victoria. After her husband, Albert, died in 1861 at the age of 42, she spent more than a decade hidden away from the public. Even after she began appearing again, she wore black for the rest of her life and much of her energy was poured into remembering her husband. You can see the Albert Memorial today in South Kensington, London. It's a bronze statue of Albert that depicts him gazing upon the Royal Albert Hall, which is also named after him.

Some people think that we lost something when we stopped marking death so publicly. After someone dies, watching the world carry on as normal feels insulting. In his book, Philip Ariès describes how, just over a hundred years ago, when someone died, a notice of bereavement would be posted on the door of the home. All the windows and doors would be closed, except the front door so that the family could welcome the many visitors. A bell would be rung to let people know what had occurred, and the funeral service would bring the whole community together. Life would return to normal 'little by little'.

Today, we no longer have established rules about how to grieve when someone dies. It's an intensely private thing that often happens behind closed doors. In his book, Ariès worries that this can leave people feeling abandoned – that, unlike in the past, people are too embarrassed or afraid to be with others in their sadness. We need to remember the Bible's instruction to 'Mourn with those who mourn.'

A Good Death

If death is the enemy, then is it possible to have a 'good' death? People certainly used to think so. In the Middle Ages they wrote documents called *Ars moriendi*, which means 'The Art of Dying'. People wanted to be prepared for death.

In recent years, a number of books have been written that could be seen as modern versions of these manuals. In his book, *Being Mortal: Illness, Medicine, and What Matters in the End*, the American surgeon Atul Gawande describes how the fight to keep death at bay at all costs means that, despite the fact that most people want to die at home, many end their lives surrounded by medical equipment and suffering from the side effects of very aggressive treatments. He wrote his book because he fears that doctors are avoiding having important conversations with patients about what they want at the end of their life, and sometimes using treatments that actually make things worse, not better.

I'm glad that my mum was able to die at home. I don't want to describe it as a good death because it was devastating. But I'm glad that she wasn't in pain, and that she didn't carry on having the harsh treatments that had already been tried, causing her hair to fall out. I'm glad that my dad was honest with me about what was happening and that I was able to spend time with her, sitting next to her on the bed, talking to her and massaging her hands with the rose-scented cream a friend had given us. I'm glad that she had visits from people who could encourage her in her faith and reassure her that she was going to be with God. In a photo that my dad took of my mum after she died, she looks as if she is smiling.

When someone dies, people often tell us that they are 'at peace'. That can be hard to hear when we are desperately wishing that they were still with us. But being 'at peace' is also an idea that we find in the Bible. Throughout the New Testament, we read about Christians not dying but 'falling asleep'.

Dr Wyatt is convinced that there is a comforting message here. So many Christians, he writes in his own book, are 'anxious and fearful about the process of dying. What will it feel like to die? Will I be struggling for breath, experiencing unbearable agony, overwhelmed with fear, sucked into a terrifying black hole of non-existence?' But what if sleeping is the best picture we have for what it is like to die? Falling asleep, he writes, 'is not something strange or terrifying; it is an experience that our heavenly Father gives us in advance so that we need not be fearful.'

I don't think I'll ever see death as a friend, but I believe that talking about it can help us to be less afraid. There are times when I can just about manage the confidence to join with Paul in celebrating Jesus' triumph over death. But there are more times when I feel overwhelmed by fear of death. At those times, it helps to remember Jesus at the grave of Lazarus, sharing our outrage at death's power, but confident that in just a few moments, he will show to those in tears around him that it is no match for his own.

Sam's Story

Sam's mother was ill for almost all of his childhood – from the time when he was 5 until her death when he was 18. When we met, he described the conversation in which she told him that she was dying as 'still probably the most vivid experience of my life'. He was 15 at the time. It was the fact that his mother had been dying for so long, rather than her death, that had the biggest impact on him:

> The dying was excruciating in lots of ways, particularly in terms of her physical pain. And by the end she looked like a scene of an Ethiopian famine. She was as thin as a rake and it was very distressing even to touch her . . . There was a level on which I wish she had lived to 80 years, but there was also a sense in which she had always been ill, and she had got to the point where she was really ill, so the idea that she might go on living like that was not heaven at all, it was terrible.

A few weeks after Sam's mother died, he had a recurring nightmare in which she came back to life. He would tell her that it would be much easier if she died, and he would close the coffin lid.

> At the time I felt very bad about it, and didn't talk to anybody about it, but actually I was right – it was much easier if she died, both for her, and for us, and there was no joy in carrying on as she was in the last few weeks.

Feelings of relief are very normal after a long illness. If it's a dream that is troubling you, it's important to remember that dreams aren't something we can control – we should never feel guilty about what happens in them. Talking to someone you trust about them can be really helpful, or simply learning that many people have dreams that disturb them. In *A Monster Calls*, a novel by Patrick Ness, Conor, whose mum is dying of cancer, has a recurring dream in which he lets her slip from his grasp as she's hanging over a cliff edge, being pulled down by a monster. He worries that this means that he wants her to die and has to learn, like Sam, that wanting someone you love not to suffer anymore is not something to feel guilty about.

After his mother became seriously ill, Sam had to grow up quite quickly, learning how to do things around the house including cooking and washing clothes. Looking back, he wishes that he had spent more time *with* his mother rather than doing things *for* her. He has come to see this as the 'big choice' in life: we can either do things for people or be with them.

He also came to believe that God was 'with us, all of us, through that experience', and in the course of our conversation, he told me about why he thinks the story in the book of Daniel about the fiery furnace is so important.

You might have read about Daniel in the lion's den – how King Darius ordered Daniel to be thrown to the lions – but what comes first in the Bible is the story of how three Jewish men – Shadrach, Meshach and Abednego – refused to worship King Nebuchadnezzar's gold statue. They were thrown into a fire as punishment, but to the King's amazement, a fourth person appeared next to them in the flames. 'Look!' Nebuchadnezzar shouted. 'I see four men, unbound, walking round in the fire unharmed! And the fourth looks like a god!' (Daniel 3:25)

'They weren't taken out of the fire. The fire wasn't put out; they didn't die in the fire,' Sam told me. 'They found God with them in the fire.'

My prayer for you today is that you would know this, too. That God does not leave us to go through anything alone but walks with us through whatever we face. I pray that, like Sam, you will one day look back on this time and know that God was with you in the fire.

CHAPTER 5
CONVERSATIONS
(& GRACE'S STORY)

> There were so many things he'd wanted to say to his mum
> and had never been able to. Now he felt urgent, as though time
> was slipping through his fingers like grains of sand.
>
> Tony in *On Eagles' Wings* by Sue Mayfield

In films, conversations with people who are dying are often dramatic. Sometimes, there is some vital piece of information that needs to be shared or a race to the scene where time is running out for a final encounter.

In the last weeks and days that my mum was alive, I don't remember her giving me any final words of advice. By then she was extremely tired, so it's hard to know whether she simply didn't have the energy or if she might have felt that I was too young for some conversations. But I wonder if there was anything left for me to say or to hear. My mum and I had always been so close; we had always told each other that we loved each other.

My memories of November 1994 are of sitting next to my mum on my parents' bed, enjoying being close to her. That last week that she was alive was the week before my 12th birthday, and I felt urgently that I needed a special, significant gift from my parents – something to help me remember. So my dad and I went out to H. M. Samuel and bought a ring – a small gold one with a heart containing a tiny diamond. I used to tell people that my mum had given it to me, even though in reality she was not well enough to give me a present, although I still have a card which she managed to scribble a line on. I wore it for years and it's even slightly bent in shape because I used to anxiously fiddle with it a lot when I was at school. The ring is much too small for me now, and I keep it in a box in my wardrobe.

Being Present

Being with someone who is dying is an intense experience and one that many people don't have to face until they are much older. I remember the contrast between the calm, competent nurses who looked after my mum, and the nervous, fearful manner of friends and relatives who came to visit. It felt as if we were suddenly operating in a different time zone to the world around us – as if a distant horizon that had occasionally come into view over the past two years was suddenly right in front of our noses. We were on the receiving end now of visits, carers, frozen meals, and so much practical concern.

I don't remember resisting the news that my mum was dying, although I do remember my horror and fear. Research suggests that this makes me a bit unusual – it's common for younger teenagers not to realize or acknowledge that a family member is dying, even when it seems obvious to those around them. A few years ago, Professor Grace Christ, a researcher, interviewed 80 families with a terminally ill parent – a study she wrote about in her book *Healing Children's Grief*. She found that many of the young people aged 12 to 14 showed 'adamant optimism by avoiding facts and feelings'. They often avoided information about their parent's illness, unlike younger children who earnestly tried to seek it out. Professor Christ learned that this behaviour was related to a desire to deny what was happening, and also to a fear that talking about the illness might lead to a loss of emotional control in front of others – often her interviewees preferred to cry alone in their room at night. While it's important to spend time with someone who is dying, it's also important to give yourself permission to taste the world outside, take an opportunity to breathe and clear your mind a bit, and focus on your own thoughts and feelings.

In his interview for the *Griefcast* podcast, the musician and cricket writer Felix White, who was 17 when his mum died of multiple sclerosis, remembers coming back elated from an Oasis concert during the final days of his mum's life. His dad later reassured him that he didn't need to beat himself up about this, telling him that 'the fact I had enjoyed myself cut through all that pain she was feeling in that moment.'

How Long?

In the final days of my mum's life, it was very clear that she would die soon. If you're at this point, or think that you might be, it can help to have your own conversation(s) with the people caring for the person you love, such as their doctors or nurses. It might not be possible for them to give you a precise idea of how long you have left, but they should be able to give you some advice. If you find face-to-face conversations difficult, you could try phoning a helpline. Many charities, such as Macmillan Cancer Support, run phone and email lines staffed by nurses who can talk through specific questions with you.

When someone is dying, their appearance is often transformed. It can be difficult to see somebody in such a vulnerable state – when they are unconscious or only faintly conscious. The contrast with their usual self can be difficult to process, particularly if they were previously very healthy, active or lively. In *The Last Act of Love*, Cathy Rentzenbrink describes having to get over her 'squeamishness' at seeing her older brother naked when she helps to wash and care for him. In *A Monster Calls*, when Conor is hugged by his mum, he notices 'her thin, thin arms that used to be so soft when she hugged him'.

Sometimes, when people are very ill, or taking strong medicines for pain, they may say things that don't make sense. I remember finding that particularly difficult in the last days of my mum's life. I was afraid that she would say something confusing or mysterious that I would never have the opportunity to ask her about. It felt as if she was slipping away from us.

Dr Hazel Gilkes, a doctor who specializes in caring for people at the end of their life, told me that if someone is slipping in and out of consciousness, you can keep talking to them: 'I always suggest assuming they can hear rather than the other way around,' she said. 'I think people who are actively dying recognize a familiar voice even if they might not understand every word.' She described how families sometimes helped to care for the person in practical ways – like when I massaged my mum's hands with hand cream. These little things can stand in for words, helping you to feel close to the person.

What to Say

Not every conversation with someone who is dying needs to be profound. You can still talk to them about very ordinary things: how your day was, what shows you've been watching, what you had for tea. Isobel Bremner, who leads the Candle Child Bereavement Service at St Christopher's Hospice, agrees that 'everyday things' are precious, and that they are also the things that can be hardest to remember. She recommends recording conversations – something that's easy to do on a smartphone or Dictaphone. If you can, try to save this somewhere safe, and as soon as you can.

Often, what needs to be said at the end of someone's life is very simple. In *On Eagles' Wings*, when Tony does manage to tell his mother what he wants to say, it's just 'I love you, Mum.' For Conor in *A Monster Calls*, it's 'I don't want you to go.'

But these things can be hard to articulate. It could be that your family isn't particularly expressive, and you're not used to talking about your feelings. Perhaps it feels artificial or forced to start now. If that's you, then it's important to remember that people express love in all sorts of ways. In a poem called 'Atlas', Ursula Fanthorpe talks about 'a kind of love called maintenance' and lists the sorts of things that this love does: remembering to plant bulbs, checking the insurance, dealing with dentists, and sending postcards. It's a good reminder of all the everyday, practical ways that we can show that we love one another – not the big gestures that we might associate with love, but the kind that are a sort of glue that binds us together. For me, it's the memory of my mum changing everyone's beds and talking about the 'fresh sheets smell', and the diary I found, years after she died, filled with notes about where she was taking us after school. After she died, I tried to pick up these habits of love.

Words aren't the only way we can express how we feel. But if there are things that have been nagging away at you, causing you to agonize over whether and when to say them to the person who is dying, it's important to find a way to resolve that. Something that might help is to write down exactly what you want to say, and practise reading it out alone or to someone you trust, to avoid everything coming out in a splurge. Praying can help too – telling God what it is that you want to say and asking for guidance about how to say it. Remember that you aren't in control of the response that you get from the person. What they say or don't say might not be exactly what you are hoping for. Although an illness can bring families together, it doesn't magically fix the stresses and strains that can shape our relationships.

Regret

Not everybody gets to have a final conversation before someone dies, or at least one they realize is final at the time. Sometimes, children and teenagers aren't told how serious an illness is. This is the case for Polly, in *Confusion*, another novel by Elizabeth Jane Howard.

After her mother has died, Polly starts piecing together clues. Why didn't she realize that her mother was dying when her brother was summoned back home early from school? She is angry about never having had a moment to be completely alone with her mother, to tell her that she would look after her dad and brothers, and to ask her mother, 'Are you alright? Can you bear to die, whatever it means?'

Will, whose story can be found at the end of Chapter 11, had no idea that the hug he shared with his mother one Sunday morning would be the last. 'My mother and I would often say, "I love you,"' he told me.

> Before I went to church that morning, we had a longer hug than
> usual, and it was really heartfelt what we said that particular
> day. Neither of us knew that she was going to die later that day.
> When I look back at that, I think God's hand was in that and
> was in that moment just before I went to church.

When he was given an opportunity to see his mother's body after she died, he was able to say a prayer and tell her that he would see her again in heaven.

It's a beautiful story. But some people are haunted by their final words, or simply regret that their last meeting or conversation wasn't what they would have wished.

At St Christopher's Hospice, Isobel Bremner often finds herself reassuring the teenagers who feel guilty about their relationship with a dead parent, telling them that their being 'challenging, and spirited, and feisty' will have reassured their parent. 'A parent who is dying wants to know that their child is going to survive without them,' she explains. 'As a parent, you look at the whole of your young person and you love all of them.'

While it's normal to remember things that you regret – fights, hurtful words, disappointments – it's important to look at a whole life, not just those moments that haunt you. We are always more than our final conversation. If there are things that you wish you had said while they were alive, it might help to write these down in a letter to the person, or to discuss with someone else what you wish you had said.

Not Alone

The last hours of a person's life are both precious and strange. I felt so disorientated in the days surrounding my mum's death, caught between what I could see happening around me and questions about what was happening in God's kingdom, in heaven. I still look back on my mum's death as the most surreal time of my life – a time when all of our beliefs about life, death and beyond were truly tested. What did it mean to say goodbye, but in the faith that it wasn't forever? Where was she going?

A Bible verse I've come to love is 1 Corinthians 13:12 (MSG):

> We can see and understand only a little about God now, as if we were peering at his reflection in a poor mirror; but some-day we are going to see him in his completeness, face-to-face. Now all that I know is hazy and blurred, but then I will see everything clearly, just as clearly as God sees into my heart right now.

For me, these words capture the weirdness of life and death. The Bible reassures us that it's the same for everyone – none of us can truly understand these things; they're too enormous. But God knows each one of us perfectly, including the person who has died. When we say goodbye to them, whether we are able to do it while they can hear it or not, we do so in the knowledge that they are going to be with a God who knows them even better than we do.

Malcolm Guite, the poet I mentioned in Chapter 4, told me that the thing that comforts him the most, when he thinks about dying, is that we don't die alone because God is with us. I hope that this is particularly reassuring for you if the person you love died on their own, or if you weren't able to be by their side. The passage that Malcolm pointed to is a famous one: Psalm 23, which begins with 'The Lord is my shepherd.' It includes these lines:

> Even though I walk
> through the valley of the shadow of death,
> I will fear no evil,
> for you are with me;
> your rod and your staff,
> they comfort me.

'Shepherds led from the front – they would take the sheep from one pasture up to the other,' Malcom told me. 'The person who wrote the Psalm is saying that God is going to walk with me through the shadow of death, ahead of me, as a shepherd, to reassure me that there is a way out of this valley.' This shepherd, Malcolm explained, is Jesus – the Jesus who experienced death himself, who told his followers 'I am the good shepherd. The good shepherd lays down his life for the sheep.' Malcolm explained:

> The thing that is most fearful to me from this side of the river as it were, was the sense of aloneness in the actual passage, of having to do it all by yourself, and not have a friend go through it with you. So that has become one of the most powerful things for me, both in my own faith and also when I am taking funerals and talking to the bereaved, that there is somebody who will be there for you and the person who died. Jesus was there, and you can constantly talk to Jesus who holds the hand of the person that you have lost.

Henri Nouwen, a Dutch priest, put it like this:

> Dying is trusting the catcher. To care for the dying is to say, 'Don't be afraid. Remember that you are the beloved child of

God. He will be there for you when you make your long jump. Don't try to grab him; he will grab you. Just stretch out your arms and hands, and trust, trust, trust.'

I know that this can be so hard to do – to trust that God really is holding the hands of the person you love. As the writer to the Corinthians put it, 'Our vision is blurred,' (1 Corinthians: 13:12) The beautiful thing is that God's sight, and catch, is flawless.

Grace's Story

I knew that I wanted to meet Grace after reading her story in the newspaper I work for. Grace had described how the loss of her mother, when Grace was seven months pregnant, had helped her to see a different side of God. It's a story about deep courage and learning that God isn't standing in anger and judgement over us.

Grace's mother died just ten weeks after being diagnosed with pancreatic cancer. Grace, who was 18 at the time, had already moved out to live with her boyfriend after an unhappy childhood at home. She had given up the five A-levels she was taking and started working as a care assistant in a nursing home.

Growing up, she had lived with the possibility that her mother, who had bipolar disorder, might take her own life. But now she found herself 20 weeks pregnant, facing the possibility that her mother might not live to see her first grandchild. Grace recalled:

I wanted to be there as much as possible. I was 18 and pregnant and quite lonely, and it was good to be around mum. It was hard sometimes, because it was very clear that mum wasn't going to live for very long.

I had always grown up knowing that there was a God, but I had fallen away from any kind of good relationship with God. I actually went through quite a big stage in my adolescence of very much feeling that God was really angry with me, particularly when I had moved out and was living with my boyfriend, and we were doing things that I knew weren't right, and I had left college. I was terrified, really, of God. My mum dying was probably one of the worst times of my life, but it really struck me that, actually, she was really comfortable – she seemed to be being looked after by God. It almost revealed to me a side of God that I hadn't recognised for a long time.

Grace's son was born two months after her mum died, and she remembers how exhausting this time was. She was learning how to care for a baby without anyone there to show her what to do, training to be a nurse, and doing all on a tiny budget. 'I was so embroiled in looking after the baby that I didn't really process a lot of the grief at that time,' she recalled. Although she wanted to go back to church, she avoided it because, as a single teenage mum, she was worried about being judged. It was only after meeting another student nurse, Gareth, who she later married, that she found the courage to go. Today, Grace is a priest herself who is passionate about welcoming people who, like her, might worry about being judged at church.

Her message for others going through what she survived is that grief is 'a very individual journey' and that going back to school and enjoying being with your friends 'doesn't mean that you love that person any less'.

'Whatever your situation is, it's your grief and the most important thing you can do is just be kind to yourself,' she advised. 'There aren't many peers that will understand what you are going through, and that will be really difficult at times because it will feel quite isolating, so if you need help from other people, then get help from other people.'

Looking back, she can see signs of God's presence in her life during the hardest moments:

When I did my training, there would be times when the rent man would be at the door and I would be hiding, or the electricity would be cut off, and I always really felt that mum was there with that, in that, somehow still there . . . I think probably God was there, but I hadn't really recognised that at the time.

CHAPTER 6
SAYING GOODBYE
(& ANDREW'S STORY)

I shift one foot to the other because my mother's shoes are too tight
and my feet hurt. I concentrate on the pain, and the blisters
that are forming on my little toes, because that way I don't have
to think about the coffin that is being lowered into the ground.
Or that my father's body is inside it.

Davey in *Tiger Eyes* by Judy Blume

I did not want to go to my mum's funeral. We had it in our church,
a modern building that stood by the side of a busy road, lined with
banners embroidered with bible verses, and normally full of families
singing, chatting, and chasing down errant toddlers. Afterwards, we
drove to the village where my mum had lived before meeting my dad,
so that she could be buried in the churchyard of the little stone church
where they had got married. It was the first funeral I had ever been to.

The sight of my mum's coffin lying on a stand at the front of our
church was horrifying to me. It wasn't that I believed that she was
still alive inside that box. It was the thought that the physical part of
my mum – the warm, soft body that had hugged me so tightly – was
going away forever. I found everything that had been done to try to
make this event beautiful, somehow – the flowers, the polished wood
of the coffin – disturbing. Everything was tainted by death. The first
thing I wanted to do when I got home was wash it all off.

I feel slightly funny about sharing that story because most of the
people I've spoken to believe that going to a funeral is an important

thing to do. It's apparently very rare for teenagers to regret going to a funeral, and I suspect that, if I hadn't gone to my mum's, I might feel sad about that now. Like a baptism or a wedding, a funeral is an ancient tradition – something humans have done for thousands of years as they've tried to make sense of death.

'The thing about a funeral is that there's a long wisdom of humanity about needing to mark these events and saying, "This is the day we say goodbye,"' Malcolm Guite, the poet-priest, told me.

I think we do need outward and visible signs of inward and spiritual things. The thing about holding a piece of earth and letting it go, or dropping a rose, is that you may not want to do that, but actually there is a letting go of the immediate closeness of everyday physical contact. Of course, you are not letting go of love.

A funeral forces you to face reality – to do something which might be healthy and necessary, but still deeply painful.

Waiting

In the days leading up to the funeral, I remember being so conscious of my mum's absence, and wondering where she was now. The house was so quiet it was as if we had survived a storm and were now surveying the devastation it had left behind.

We weren't at home when the funeral director came to collect my mum's body. My dad took us to St Alban's cathedral, where we went to a small chapel and lit a candle. I think this was the first time that I ever saw my dad cry. I have a vivid memory of a woman – a complete stranger – giving us five pounds to take to the café, and thinking that this was so kind and unusual. (How often do people tend to look away, awkwardly, when they see people crying in public?) When we got home, two of my mum's friends had left the house clean and tidy, and smelling of flowers. I thought a bit about the women who cared for Jesus' body when he died, and how, thousands of years later, there were still women in the Church doing this precious act for their friends.

In some traditions, it's usual to spend much longer with the person who has died – something that is sometimes called a *wake*. It's changed over the course of history, and looks different depending on the country and culture you're in. In Ireland, for example, it used to be common to spend the time eating, drinking, and celebrating the life of the person. My friend Nadim Nassar, a Syrian priest in the Church of England, described to me how, at home, it was traditional for bereaved families to open their home for four or five days, so that large numbers of friends and relatives could visit to give their condolences.

I learned a few years ago that the Jewish community has a tradition called *sitting Shiva*, which takes place for seven days after someone has died (Jewish people are usually buried within 24 hours of dying). During these seven days, the immediate family is supported in their grief by friends and other family members who come to sit with them.

I was interested to read an online guide to this tradition at Shiva. com which suggested that visitors should 'typically avoid initiating conversations'. Instead, they should 'generally listen and offer support only when engaged'. Perhaps there is something to be learned from this tradition. The days after someone dies are strange, sad and lonely, and sometimes it's enough for our friends and families to simply be with us, rather than struggling to make conversation or find the right words.

In Public

One of the reasons I found my mum's funeral so difficult is that I felt very territorial about my family, and our grief. I felt as if nobody should be allowed to be grieving as much as we were; it wasn't *their* mum who had died. I also didn't like the sensation of being watched, particularly as my dad wasn't coping very well at the time. The prospect of being 'on show' can be terrifying if you long for privacy or hate the thought of your emotions spilling out in public. I've sometimes wondered if this is related to our more reserved culture of mourning, here in the UK.

'People go to the church very solemn, they have a reception afterwards, and it's more relaxed,' Nadim observed, when I asked him how our traditions compare to those in his home country.

> In the Middle East, it's like the story of Lazarus: [people are] wailing and crying and screaming. This self-expression is much more outward than [it is] here . . . Being passionate, being emotional, being impulsive – we express ourselves in a more emotional way.

He was quick to say that he didn't think this was a 'better' way of mourning, but it's a helpful reminder that there is no 'one way' that people grieve at funerals. Several of the people I interviewed struggled to remember the funeral clearly – it had passed 'in a blur'.

As much as you can, try to not worry about other people's perceptions or to study your own reaction. You might even find, looking around you, that the people gathered offer some sort of comfort. Sam, whose story we looked at in Chapter 4, remembers the small church being full to bursting for his mother's funeral. 'A lot of her life was really difficult,' he told me. 'And yet here were these 400 people who were all there to say, "Her life really mattered to me." I found that extraordinarily helpful.'

On the Day

To find out more about funerals, I decided to speak to Andrew Lightbown, the rector of a church in the countryside, not too far from London. Andrew's church has a very large churchyard, and the last time I was visiting, I noticed how kind he was to a family visiting a grave, quietly saying hello and making them feel welcome. Andrew also knows what it's like to lose a parent. You can read his story at the end of this chapter.

Andrew believes that we go to funerals to do three things. 'Firstly, we come to grieve and mourn because death is always painful and I want to acknowledge that from the pulpit, especially when it's premature,' he told me. 'It feels unjust and not right. Secondly, we come to give thanks for a life.' When it comes to this aspect, he added, 'We have to remember the whole of a life, not just the tough bits at the end.' And 'Thirdly, we come to express hope. This isn't the end.' It's the priest's job, Andrew believes, to hold these three things – grieving, hoping and remembering – together.

'The worry that teenagers have is that this is going to be just all grief, all horrible, all beyond "my ability to cope with pain,"' he told me. 'I try to explain that that's going to be part of it, but not the whole part. I will never let one cloud dominate the others.'

Something he often advises young people to think about is bringing a friend to sit with them. 'I'm very aware that the act of walking into church as a family member is difficult,' he explained.

That is a deeply uncomfortable thing to do because everyone is watching you, and they pity you, and there is that great outpouring of solidarity. But there is an intensity about being the focus of that that, in some ways, it is incredibly difficult to get.

Funerals are 'strange things', he observed:

You will feel a mixture of emotions if you come. There will be the sadness, but you will probably find yourself laughing or smiling at some point as someone says something that just captures mum or dad, or talks about a family memory or holiday, or something that just makes you laugh. And you will also carry a sense of questioning, and, hopefully, hope, and all those things will mingle together.

There are several ways in which you can have a say in what happens during a funeral, reflecting what you think the person wanted, and what you want to include. Sometimes, families choose to include a tribute or eulogy (a word that means 'high praise'). This can be read out loud by the priest or whoever is leading the funeral – you can send them as much information as you like about the person, to help them write something that captures the person you loved and how you feel about them. If you are considering reading it aloud yourself, Andrew advises thinking about how hard that might be on the day. It's because of this that he asks people who plan to speak to give him a copy of their words in advance, so that if at any point they realize they can't go through with it, he can immediately help.

'I will say to teenagers in particular, "You just have to nod at me, anytime,"' he told me. 'I will absolutely make sure I am in their eyeline the whole time. I also make the point that they don't *have* to do it.'

There are other ways that you can be involved in a funeral, he points out. You might want to ask that a particular piece of music can be played (it doesn't have to be a hymn), or a poem or a passage from a book be read aloud.

'I am the resurrection and the life.'

Sometimes, there are disagreements within families about whether a funeral should be religious or not. That can be particularly difficult to deal with, whatever your own preference is. You may feel that religious members of your family are 'imposing' faith onto you, or on the person who has died. Or you may desperately want a religious service and feel upset or angry that it will be a secular one. It may help to read Chapter 11, which has ideas about how you can remember the person you love in your own way. Many people find it helpful to write a letter to the person, and sometimes they place it with them in the coffin.

In my own case, I was very glad that my mum had a Christian funeral and burial because underpinning all of it was the faith that death was not the end. I like the fact that the Church of England's funerals website (<https://churchofenglandfunerals.org/>) gives a prominent place to the word 'hope'. There are lots of different Bible verses that might be included in a funeral service. One of Andrew's favourites is the bit in John 14, in which Jesus comforts his disciples, telling them that 'My Father's house has many rooms' and that he is 'going there to prepare a place for you'. Another passage that is often read is from John 11, which tells the story of Jesus raising Lazarus from the dead: 'I am the resurrection and the life. The one who believes in me will live, even though they die; and whoever lives by believing in me will never die.'

A religious service will also include prayers. Andrew also told me that these can help us to be honest about the complexity of relationships. 'Life isn't always necessarily plain sailing in relationships,' he explained. One of the lines that he loves in the prayers said in the Church of England is 'Heal the memories of hurt and failure,' which he tends to soften to 'any memories of hurt and failure'. It's a reminder that we can be honest in what we say to God, who already knows everything about our relationships, and the mixed-up feelings we may be holding onto at a funeral.

Final Goodbye

Most people today have a cremation rather than a burial. This can be the hardest part of the day. 'There's something incredibly final about shutting the curtains,' Andrew told me.

For my mum, we had a burial service and watched the coffin being lowered into the ground. This can be a disturbing sight, too. In Elizabeth Jane Howard's book, *Confusion*, Polly finds it 'impossible not to think of a body as a person who needed air and light'.

In both cases, words can help. In the Church of England the words that are immediately spoken when the body is taken away – either with the closing of the curtains at a crematorium or with the lowering into the grave at a burial – are 'In sure and certain hope of the resurrection to eternal life'. There is a certain strength in those words. I think of them as a sort of strong tree that we can take shelter under, even when our own worries and doubts make it difficult to understand what we have heard.

Gravestones and Ashes

It was years before I returned to the churchyard where my mum was buried. During that time, my dad couldn't face arranging for a tombstone to be designed and put up, and I worried regularly about this. I was very anxious that the grave would be 'lost' somehow. Eventually, my dad found the strength to design a beautiful stone, and I learned at this time that it's not unusual for families to not ask for one until many years after the person has died. I was also reassured to learn that the people responsible for burial sites like churchyards do have records of each grave – there was no need for me to have been so worried over the years about that. It's also common for families not to collect ashes after a cremation, sometimes for decades, or for families to struggle to decide if they want to keep or scatter the ashes, and if so, where. My favourite account of a scattering comes at the end of *Grief is the Thing with Feathers*, Max Porter's long poem about a family coping with the death of the mother. At a beach, the dad finally releases her ashes, and he and his sons yell into the wind: 'I LOVE YOU I LOVE YOU I LOVE YOU'

By the time I finished writing this book, I felt I understood more about why my mum's funeral had been so unbearable for me. I wasn't ready to let her go, and I felt deeply confused about what had happened to her. What was it that we had said goodbye to? Why did any of it matter, if she was still alive, somewhere, with God?

These are the questions we'll turn to next.

Andrew's Story

Andrew was 19 when he rang home from university to be told by his mum that his dad had died. There were no signs the day before that this was a possibility, although his dad had had an alcohol problem for many years.

'I remember feeling numb, really numb, and feeling really upset that I felt numb and didn't cry at first, thinking I should have this huge outburst, which didn't happen,' Andrew told me. 'It did eventually, but not at the time.'

Although not all will lose a parent as a result, many young people in the UK have a parent who drinks too much. The National Association of Children of Alcoholics (NACOA) estimates that it's around one in five. NACOA has an excellent website offering support,[1] and the important reminder that 'Your mum or dad's drinking is not, and never was, your fault.'

Andrew's dad's drinking was a 'family secret'. He remembers 'huge unpredictability' at home, and times when his dad had to be hospitalized. But even while others knew about this situation, it was never talked about and no mention was made of it at the funeral.

'Grieving can be long and complicated when life has been chaotic,' Andrew observed. He had had an argument over the phone with his dad the night before he died. 'I think there was a period of extreme anger, and possibly even hatred, for what had happened before, and also a sense of "How dare you leave me?"' he told me.

> There was a period where I was just not able to focus and probably went off the rails myself in quite a big way . . . There was a bizarre period of a long time of feeling "I still have to justify and prove myself to my dad," even though he wasn't there to validate whether I had done anything to get that approval or otherwise.

---

1 https://www.nacoa.org.uk/young-people

Eventually he came to feel 'compassion and sorrow', recognizing that his father would have been 'in a shed-load of pain'. He sees his dad's struggle with alcohol as an illness, 'an attempt to fill a hole in his life'.

'It's complicated, because somebody who's in that state knows the havoc they are causing, but does not want to cause that havoc,' he told me.

Very few people actually want to go in and start hurting other people, and so then it gets worse because then they feel the guilt about what's happening. But they only know one way to deal with guilt and pain [drink], so you create this kind of toxic and never-ending circle . . . I think there was a huge sense of guilt with him because he knew he was letting us down. And he didn't know how to handle that.

Andrew's experience growing up has left him with an awareness that 'we live in a world where darkness and light coalesce,' he told me. Even amid the chaos of his dad's illness, he remembers good times – it was not that his dad's ability to be kind, funny and warm disappeared. 'There were horrible things, truly horrible things,' he recalled. 'But I would still say there was God's goodness in him somewhere.'

It has also made Andrew realize that there are consequences to how we behave, that 'how we are does impact other people deeply.' Ultimately, he found that God was there in times of suffering, but he's also had times of 'real anger' at God, asking, 'Why me? Why have you allowed this?' At one point he wrote a letter to God, putting down on paper exactly what he thought, and posted it – an idea I immediately loved. I asked him what advice he would have for someone going through a similar experience. 'Absolutely, this is not your fault,' he replied. This is also the message from NACOA, which created the Six Cs: 'I didn't **cause** it; I can't **control** it; I can't **cure** it; I can take **care** of myself; I can **communicate** my feelings; I can make healthy **choices**.'

'If you are able to find a way of talking about the truth about this at an earlier stage than I was able to, that might help,' Andrew adds. In the past, he was tempted to gloss over the years on his CV that followed his dad's death when he found himself struggling to cope, but today he sees it less as a 'secret to be hidden' than 'something that can be redeemed, maybe not totally redeemed this side of heaven, but partially redeemed'.

As our conversation came to a close, I wondered whether part of that redemption might be the care that Andrew now offers to grieving families at his church, remembering his promise to stay in the eyeline of teenagers reading out eulogies at funerals, ready to jump in at any moment. He understands because he's been there.[2]

---

2 You can find more information, including the stories of young people affected by alcoholism in the family, and phone and email helplines at <https://www.nacoa.org.uk/young-people.html.>

CHAPTER 7
WHAT HAPPENS
WHEN WE DIE?
(& CARRIE'S STORY)

> What happens to her? I mean has she just stopped? Or has she gone
> somewhere else? It may seem idiotic to you, but the whole
> thing – death, you know, and all that – I can't think what it is.
> Simon, to his sister, Polly, in *Confusion*
> by Elizabeth Jane Howard

A few years ago, for a report entitled 'No Questions Asked', the charity Youthscape did some interviews with people aged 14 to 16. They wanted to find out what this group thought about God. Interestingly, without being prompted by the interviewer, all those who took part brought up the subject of death. One of the questions most commonly raised was 'What happens after we die?'

Losing someone can force you to confront this question for the first time. In Jeff Zentner's novel *Goodbye Days*, Carver, who has lost three friends in a car accident, describes himself as 'a casual believer in God':

> My belief has never been tested in this way. I've never had to examine myself to decide whether I *truly* believe that my friends are currently in the presence of some benevolent and loving God. What if there is no God? Where are they? What if they're each locked in some huge white marble room with blank walls, and they're there for eternity with nothing to do, nothing to see, nothing to read, nobody to talk to?

Confusion

A major difference between the UK today and the UK that grieving people of the past inhabited is that far fewer people believe in God or life after death. There is no longer one set of beliefs that unites us – the way that we talk about death varies enormously.

After my mum died, I thought intensely about where she was and what she was doing. I didn't consider the possibility that she had simply stopped existing. The thought that she had one minute been alive and present – full of thoughts, dreams and experiences – and in the next, had just ceased to be didn't seem believable. Yet I didn't feel I had a clear idea about what had happened to her.

Some of what I heard about heaven made me feel guilty because it didn't sound like a place where I would want to spend eternity. I think I feared that heaven would be one long worship service where the band never stopped repeating a chorus.

Finding answers to my questions hasn't been easy. In his book, *The Beauty and the Horror*, Richard Harries, a former Bishop of Oxford, wrote that, for many Christians, life after death has 'almost dropped out of active consideration altogether'. Like me, he can't remember hearing a sermon on it. Harries' theory is that today we are so afraid of 'wishful thinking', that 'we find it difficult to believe that there really could be any such reality as glorious as heaven.' But, he goes on to say, just because something is comforting doesn't make it untrue – we should be 'sceptical about an approach that states almost as a matter of definition that anything that consoles is unreal'. In fact, he argues, 'Hope in the face of death is an essential element of Christian belief', not an optional extra.

This wouldn't have been news to the early Christians. In his book, *A Brief History of Heaven*, Alister McGrath, once an atheist scientist and now a professor of science and religion at Oxford, describes how ideas about heaven have developed over the centuries. It's through our imagination, he suggests, that humans grapple with the idea of heaven – something we will never truly be able to comprehend this side of it. Some have spoken of it as a home to which we will return, like William Wordsworth, a 19th century poet who described how 'Trailing clouds of glory do we come / From God who is our home.' My dad tells me that this was one of my mum's favourite quotations.

Search for Answers

As a teenager, the Bible passage I turned to most often was 1 Thessalonians 4 (NIV):

> Brothers and sisters, we do not want you to be uninformed about those who sleep in death, so that you do not grieve like the rest of mankind, who have no hope. For we believe that Jesus died and rose again, and so we believe that God will bring with Jesus those who have fallen asleep in him. According to the Lord's word, we tell you that we who are still alive, who are left until the coming of the Lord, will certainly not precede those who have fallen asleep. For the Lord himself will come down from heaven, with a loud command, with the voice of the archangel and with the trumpet call of God, and the dead in Christ will rise first. After that, we who are still alive and are left will be caught up together with them in the clouds to meet the Lord in the air. And so we will be with the Lord forever. Therefore encourage one another with these words.

The words that I clung to were 'caught up together' (these are the ones that we eventually chose for the headstone on my mum's grave); I thought about me, my dad, my mum, my brother and sister all being reunited. But the passage also sounded so fantastical. Could it really be true?

A few years ago, Professor Tom Wright, a bishop in the Church of England, wrote a book called *Surprised by Hope*. He had come to think that many people, including Christians, didn't really know what the 'ultimate Christian hope' was. He wanted to remind people of what the very first Christians believed. These Christians didn't speak about 'going to heaven' when they died. Instead, they believed that their bodies would one day be resurrected. Just as Jesus had returned from the dead in a transformed body that people could see and touch, we, too, will be given new bodies. This, Professor Wright says, is the truth. We've just forgotten it.

In the Bible, the Book of Philippians puts it this way:

> There's far more to life for us. We're citizens of high heaven! We're waiting the arrival of the Saviour, the Master, Jesus Christ, who will transform our earthy bodies into glorious bodies like his own. He'll make us beautiful and whole with the same powerful skill by which he is putting everything as it should be, under and around him. (Philippians 3:20–21, MSG).

I love to imagine my mum not as she was in the final weeks before she died, but with a body that is 'beautiful and whole'. Yet this account raises all sorts of questions about how resurrection might actually work. After all, billions of people have died and we know that after we die, our bodies decompose. This isn't a new worry – even in the second century people were asking anxious questions about it. An explanation I found helpful comes from another famous Christian scientist, Professor John Polkinghorne. He describes it in computer terms: who we are is like software which God can download and save, until he gives us new hardware on which to run the software. We are like a code that God will never forget.

The idea of being held in God's memory is one that another professor, John Swinton, has written about. John is the founder of the University of Aberdeen's Centre for Spirituality, Health and Disability and in his wonderful book about dementia, *Living in the Memories of God*, he writes: 'To be human is to be held in the memory of God. God watches over human beings, knows them intimately, and remembers them.'

I particularly love his words because they reassure us that God will always remember those we love – a helpful message, particularly if you worry about your own memories fading. Everything that was special, remarkable, funny and unique about our loved ones is perfectly preserved by the One who made them.

More Than Harp Playing

In *The Spying Game*, Pat Moon's novel about the fallout from a fatal car crash, Joe, the son of the victim, says: 'What bothers me, if there is a heaven, is what Dad's going to do all day. What he really liked was mending things: clocks, toaster, toys, hairdryers.'

One of the things I like about Tom Wright's writing is that he paints an exciting picture of a future that includes those who have died. He encourages us to see that we are part of a bigger story, and that those we love, including those who have died, are part of it, too. This is the story of the remaking of heaven and earth. We get a glimpse of this in Revelation 21, where the writer describes hearing a loud voice saying:

> Look! Look! God has moved into the neighbourhood, making his home with men and women! They're his people, he's their God. He'll wipe every tear from their eyes. Death is gone for good – tears gone, crying gone, pain gone – all the first order of things gone.' (Revelation 21: 3-5, MSG)

It's hard to imagine such a world, but God's promise is that this is our ultimate destination: a new earth joined with a new heaven. To some people, this might sound surprising. Sometimes we get the idea that the earth is a dark, sinful place that we get to escape by getting to heaven. But the Bible tells us, right at the beginning, that when God created the world, he saw that it was good. His long-term plan is not to destroy it, but to remake it.

Our destiny isn't to go 'up' to heaven and stay there forever. Instead, we are expecting Jesus to come back to earth to renew it.

Tom's Wright's explanation of my favourite passage – the one about being gathered up in the clouds – is that those who are still alive on earth when Jesus comes back to renew the world will go to greet him and escort him here, like the citizens of a country welcoming a returning ruler.

And he has encouraging words for those who are worried that heaven will be boring. In this new, remade world, we will all have a part to play: 'Far from sitting on clouds playing harps, as people often imagine . . . [We] will be agents of his love going out in new ways, to accomplish new creative tasks, to celebrate and extend the glory of his love.'

Where Is She Now?

But what does this mean for those who have died before Jesus returns, before we are all resurrected? On the cross, Jesus reassured the thief who was crucified next to him that 'Today you will be with me in paradise.' Tom Wright explains that *paradise* means 'not a final destination, but the blissful garden, the parkland of rest and tranquillity, where the dead are refreshed as they await the dawn of the new day.' Those who are dead are 'held firmly within the conscious love of God and the conscious presence of Jesus Christ.'

Sometimes, our beliefs about what happens when we die change over time. Joanna Collicutt told me that she now feels much more confident than she used to about reassuring people that they would see the person they loved again.

'I used to say when I was not sure about this, "God will give you your heart's desire,"' she explained.

I now think I would quite happily say more than that. I say that the person is in God's gaze, still existing, and we will be with the Lord together eventually . . . That is often our heart's desire and God only wishes good things for us. And this is so fundamental to who we are.'

She suggests looking back right to the beginning of the Bible: 'The first thing God says after he has created Adam is it's not good that the man should be alone. I think that tells us that in the redemption of all things we will be with those we love.'

My own belief is that our love for one another is something that delights God, an echo of his own endless, unconditional love for us. I believe that, like the prodigal son who's met by his father in the road, there are many people waiting to greet us and celebrate with us when we come home to him. I also take comfort from the fact that death is a journey that others, including my mum, have made before me. I like to think of the 'great cloud of witnesses' that the Bible talks about in Hebrews, cheering me on through life, and waiting for me when mine ends. Ultimately, I have come to focus on who I think God is, rather than the exact details of what this destination might be like. Dante Alighieri, an Italian writer who wrote the famous *The Divine Comedy*, described God as 'the love that moves the sun and the other stars'. I believe that he understands my longing to see my mum again and that this is a hope I can trust him with.

Worries About Where They Are

Another worry that people have is that the person they love might not go to be with God because they were not a Christian while they were alive. Debate over this question has raged over the centuries, and it still has the power to cause serious disagreements among Christians. Some are convinced that unless people profess a faith in Jesus before they die, they are destined to go to hell – so convinced that they urgently preach warnings, even on the streets. Others do not believe that our last opportunity to encounter God's grace is on our deathbed.

Those who hold the latter opinion include Malcolm Guite, the poet-priest we met earlier. He believes that dying means 'meeting your maker'. He thinks of it as a moment of revelation:

Everybody who steps out of this life sees the face of God in Jesus Christ and realises, now [that] the lights are on, that the person who was holding their hands in the dark, who led them through the dark passage, the valley of the shadow of death, is the same Jesus who is looking at them.

I asked him what he says to those who tell him that the person they love, who has died, was an atheist. He replied:

I would probably say, "Your friend is meeting their maker and their maker loves your friend." The God to whom they have gone not only loves that person but loves that person just as much and more than you do. And if there is anything you want that's good for that person now, you can bet their maker wants it too.

'It's not that we are not judged after we die,' he added. 'I believe when we look at ourselves in the light of God's astonishing love, of course we will see all the stuff we did wrong.' Lots of people in the Bible were transformed by such light, he points out. We will all have a choice too:

His grace will enable us, if we want to, to let go of all that was wrong and just to lean on his mercy and accept the offer of grace and life. But I also think that we have the freedom to turn away, to say no.

Andrew, who shared his story about his dad in the last chapter, told me:

I am just forever hopeful. I believe that, as the Bible puts it, 'in my father's house there are many dwelling places'. I don't know what was in my dad's heart . . . I have no idea what he may have been praying, feeling, communicating to God. But I would be immensely surprised if it wasn't something, and I do believe God is merciful, God is just . . . I think it's alright. I have a feeling it's okay.

This is also my belief, strengthened by the Bible stories that remind us that God goes after those that are lost, desiring to bring them safely home.

Trusting

Writing this book has been harder than I thought it might be. It has forced me to think more about what happened during my teenage years and about the fears that I've carried with me. Sometimes I still struggle to believe in something as incredible as the resurrection and the return of Jesus. I think it's particularly hard in a country like England, where most people around you don't share this belief.

In her book *A Tour of Bones: Facing Fear and Looking for Life*, the writer Denise Inge wrote about resurrection:

It is not so much about believing the impossible but believing that, because our knowledge is limited, there may be many possibilities of which we have not conceived . . . It is the daring act of staking a claim in the unprovable . . . It is audacious.

Today I choose to be audacious.

Carrie's Story

Two weeks after her 19th birthday, Carrie was called at university by her mother and sister. Her dad had been hit by a car while on his regular morning bike ride and killed.

Looking back, she thinks it was a full ten years before she was able to really process what had happened, including her fears about her own role in it. Just a few months before her dad was killed, she had been to the funeral of the mum of a school friend and written in her journal that the hardest loss to bear would be the death of her dad 'because we'd had such a difficult relationship'. When he did die, she believed that in some way, she had caused it. She also had an 'eerie' feeling that it had been a premonition, and she found herself asking, 'Was this some sort of cruel trick? Like God had heard me say that this would be the hardest loss, so then it happened?' She scratched out the entry in her journal and tore the page out.

It was a 'tremendous release' when, in her late 20s, she confessed this fear to her therapist, who told her that, no, nothing she had done had caused her dad's death, that 'some things in life are just coincidences.' Today, she no longer looks for patterns in the circumstances of his death, she says. 'There is more of an acceptance that it happened.'

Carrie's stormy relationship with her dad made the grief 'more complicated', she told me.

> I couldn't even touch it for a really long time. I would lie to people about my dad's death . . . And if I did acknowledge his death it was always in the context of 'We were really close; it was such a hard loss.'

Because her Dad had been a prominent figure in the community, the press came to the funeral and to a candlelit vigil for which people flooded the streets. It was strange for her to see her dad venerated, knowing that he was also someone who had 'a lot of weaknesses'. It was after a year of therapy that Carrie began to be able to acknowledge that 'actually it was a very difficult relationship and he died'. She had to learn to hold these two truths together.

Something I found fascinating was Carrie's understanding of how our relationships with our parents change, even after they have died. As we enter adulthood, we start seeing them less as two-dimensional characters who are either bad or good, but as complex individuals. 'We see the struggles that they went through and their shortcomings, the mistakes that they made, but also the beautiful things that they did, and we accept them more as a whole person,' she observed.

I asked her what she believed about life after death. 'From the very beginning I was certain that there is some sort of afterlife, and I think that the wall between this world and that world is quite thin,' she told me. She has also experienced a number of 'supernatural' things since her dad died, including, in the first six months, seeing a male figure (not her dad), who told her 'Everything is going to be okay. You are going to make it through this.' She said she didn't feel scared, just 'really calm and at peace'.

Having worried in the past about whether she was doing grief 'right', her advice today is to 'trust the grieving process – you are grieving even if you don't feel like you are . . . If you need to cry, cry. If you need to not talk about it, don't talk about it.'

Going to a grief support group was 'tremendously helpful', she said, as was talking to a friend who had lost a brother. 'Just knowing that other people had been through this and had survived it, and that I would survive it too.' She was also 'very kind' to herself, speaking words of encouragement after small victories, telling herself 'You are grieving and you are also getting dressed. That's huge. Well done!'

She told me that seeing her dad's life 'cut short' has made her live life with 'urgency':

On the one hand, it's good because you have this awareness, but on the other hand, I know I do need to relax a little bit. I am aware though of things my dad wanted to do and didn't do, and I don't want that to be my story so it's a very difficult tension to live in.

Right after she lost her dad, Carrie told her best friend that she didn't think she would ever be happy again. She told me:

The advice I would give is that I can sit here now and say, 'You will be happy again.' It's absolutely shocking the way that the heart can heal, and the way that you can recover and thrive in the midst of tremendous pain. Better days really do lie ahead, and I know that it doesn't feel like it right now, because it didn't to me either, but if you can even have a tiny shred of that hope, then that's going to get you through.

CHAPTER 8
HOW COULD GOD LET THIS HAPPEN? (& DAN'S STORY)

I covet their innocence, their easy belief. They trust the world;
they trust God. They see Him everywhere. Like I did, my whole life,
and I didn't even know to appreciate how good I had it.
Lucy 'Bird' Hansson in *The Names They Gave Us*
by Emery Lord

A few years ago, I found myself in angry tears during an evening church service. The focus had shifted to prayers for healing, and hearing the good news that God had relieved someone of an earache felt not only insulting, but cruel. Had nobody thought how this might sound to those of us whose prayers for much more serious problems had seemingly gone unanswered?

I don't think that the death of my mum ever caused me to doubt the existence of God. Perhaps because both of my parents had lost a parent at a young age, I didn't grow up with the idea that we lived in a protective bubble. If there was a verse that summed up my understanding of how God and life worked, it was probably the one my dad later pinned up in our kitchen: 'In this world you will have trouble. But take heart! I have overcome the world.' My mum's death, however, did leave me with some big, troubling questions about God. C. S. Lewis once wrote that, after his wife died, he wasn't worried that he would stop believing in God, but that he would start to believe 'dreadful things' about God. He started to worry that God wasn't good.

For me, certain accounts of God's creation just made things worse.

Question: Why do bad things happen?

Answer: Because God gave us free will and humans chose to disobey him. We live in a fallen world.

Question: Then why did God create a world where that was a possibility?

Answer: Because he wanted us to choose to love and obey him, not to force us.

Question: Does that really outweigh all the terrible, sad things in the world?

At its crudest level it could sound as if my mum had to die because, many moons ago, someone had given into temptation and eaten an apple.

I also began to expect other things to go wrong: What if the reason my dad was late getting home was that he had been killed in a car crash? What if the spot on my arm was actually cancer? There was no guarantee that God *wouldn't* allow those things to happen. My prayers, particularly those offered at night when I felt most worried, didn't seem to lessen my anxiety, because my prayers hadn't 'worked' in the past.

Looking back, I think I was lucky that nobody attempted to explain what God was 'doing' through my mum's death. Other people are not so fortunate. Greg Boyd, an American pastor, describes in his book *Is God to Blame?* how Melanie, a woman whose daughter died in childbirth, had been taught that God was trying to teach her something through this awful experience. 'Do you really believe that God kills babies to teach parents a lesson?' he asked her. 'Can you picture Jesus doing that to someone?'

Why?

Sometimes called 'the problem of evil', the question of why God permits bad things to happen is an ancient one. If God is all-powerful, all-knowing and entirely good, then why does evil exist?

Naomi, Carrie's sister, who spoke to me about the sudden death of their father, remembers lying in bed and praying: 'I told God that I had trusted him, [but] he had betrayed me, and I would never allow myself to trust him again.' Although her beliefs changed over the years, she remembers that, as a teenager (and daughter of a pastor), she had to put up a 'front' in church, pretending that she felt a faith she didn't, which caused her to feel shame and guilt.

Marilyn McCord Adams, an American priest and philosopher, came to the conclusion that attempting to provide explanations about how God could allow 'horrendous evils' was not only futile but dangerous. The arguments that people came up with belittled the awfulness of what had happened to people and left them with a distorted picture of God that placed far too much of the blame on humans. Rather than asking 'Why did God allow this?' she focused on another question: 'How does God's goodness outweigh evil?' We'll return to this later.

Chaos

When I asked Paul Fiddes, a baptist minister who teaches theology in Oxford, how the death of his young son, who took his own life after struggling with mental illness, had impacted his faith, he told me that it had confirmed, rather than changed, his beliefs. 'I hadn't for a long time had an interventionist view of God who manipulates human events and therefore could be said to be directly responsible for the death of my son,' he said. 'I regarded God as equally bereft and sorrowful about the loss of a human life as I was.' Paul's understanding is that the terrible things that happen in the world are not God's intention, but one of the consequences of a world that has been given freedom by God. It's a world that is 'slipping away from the purpose of God', where chaos, accidents and tragedies are all possibilities. Although this doesn't answer all of our questions – we might ask, for example, why God chose to create a universe with such freedom – Paul believes that none of this evil is 'God's deliberate intention'.

Listening to him, I realized that this is also my belief, my intuition about the world. Something *is* terribly wrong and if God really is an all-loving being, then he cannot be behind it. Something else must be.

Talking about forces of good and evil can feel strange today. In the West, at least, we get used to speaking about our world in very practical terms: my mum died because of a disease; because we didn't catch it earlier; because we haven't yet found a medicine to cure or prevent breast cancer. But if we look at the Bible, we find a different story, one in which there really are forces working against God; one in which a spiritual battle is going on. In the Book of Hebrews, it says that Jesus died to 'break the power of him who holds the power of death'.

'The world looks like a war zone because it *is* a war zone,' writes Greg Boyd. 'God is at war with forces that oppose his will.'

Even if we find it hard to talk in these terms in everyday life, these ideas continue to bubble up in fiction. You can find it in the books we read and the films and TV we watch. Think of *Star Wars*, J. K. Rowling's *Harry Potter* books or Philip Pullman's *His Dark Materials*. That life is an adventure in which we will encounter good and evil forces is an ancient idea that still seems to help us make sense of our lives. I think I'm drawn to it because it recognizes that it takes courage to live in this world.

It's the vision of the world that we find in the Narnia books by C. S. Lewis, in which a 'deeper magic' ultimately overcomes evil. These books also remind us that, far from being behind the evil that happens to us, God opposes it and grieves over it.

In *The Magician's Nephew*, Digory, whose mother is seriously ill at home, asks the lion, Aslan, 'But please, please – won't you – can't you give me something that will cure Mother?'

Lewis, whose own mother died of cancer when he was nine, writes:

> Up till then he had been looking at the Lion's great front feet and the huge claws on them; now, in his despair, he looked up at its face. What he saw surprised him as much as anything in his whole life. For the tawny face was bent down near his own and (wonder of wonders) great shining tears stood in the Lion's eyes. They were such big, bright tears compared with Digory's own that for a moment he felt as if the Lion must really be sorrier about his Mother than he was himself.

It's a picture that I've clung to over the years because it reminds me that my mum's illness and death didn't come from God. When Jesus came across people who were sick or dying, he healed them, without exception: a sign of the 'deeper magic' at work in the world.

Powerless to Act?

If the world is a chaotic battleground, then is God simply a source of comfort and sympathy? Is God powerless to act? This seems at odds with what we read about the Bible, where we read stories of an almighty God causing and responding to events on earth, and commanding us to pray. Despite what happened to my mum, I do still pray to God when someone is ill, or when I'm worried about my own health. I see it as co-operating with God in his desire to heal and make whole.

All sorts of things can happen, including miracles, Paul Fiddes told me, but only through the 'power of persuasive love' – the force through which God acts in the world. 'When we pray for someone we are loving them, and that love of ours becomes part of God's love,' he explained. 'You could say it reinforces God's love. That may result in transformation and healing, but it may not. I would say God's purpose is always for healing, so God experiences frustration in lack of healing just as we do.'

The problem is that there are barriers to God's will that remain a mystery to us, 'all sorts of causes we know nothing about', as Paul explained. Our prayers *are* effective, because God created a world in which we can co-operate with him to bring about healing. But we also need to be aware of the 'vastness and complexity of the cosmos', as Greg Boyd puts it. The forces opposing God are not just human evil, but spiritual evil that remains hidden from us.

The outcome of this battle is not in doubt – we know that the death and resurrection of Jesus was a 'death blow' to this evil. But for now, we live in an in-between time, in which there are still casualties, including Paul's son and my mum.

Losing My Religion

I feel very aware of how empty all this may sound if you're in the midst of grief. As much as I want to share the ideas that have helped me the most, I know from experience that other people's attempts to make sense of the world, and of God, can be infuriating.

In the quote I used at the start of this chapter, Lucy 'Bird' Hansson relays the envy she feels towards those who have retained their trust in God. Her father is a local Methodist pastor, and the return of her mother's illness causes her to question God – she begins to give him the 'cold shoulder', ceasing the prayers that she has said devotedly since her childhood. 'Something that has always been as easy as speaking now feels like reciting lines,' she reflects.

My Syrian friend, Nadim, now a priest in the Church of England, grew up during a civil war in Lebanon, and when he was 18, he saw a close friend shot dead. He told me:

> I was furious with God, with life. And it's not wrong, it's not something to be ashamed of. God understands. Don't worry about God. Worry about you . . . Let God be God. Let you be you . . . But remember, you do not direct your anger to somebody who is not there . . . Let God respond to that.

Sometimes, Christians react to those who question, doubt or walk away from their faith as tragic, deluded or simply rebellious troublemakers. Churches can be hard places to be when you are full of doubt, disappointment or anger. We know that losing someone doesn't always strengthen people's faith in God. Sanderson Jones, who set up an 'atheist church' in London, The Sunday Assembly, could not comprehend why God would allow the death of his mother. This, as he describes it, 'cataclysmic catastrophic event' happened when he was just 10.

'Losing faith meant that she had to die twice,' he told an American news channel.

> Once when she went to heaven, and then when I realized heaven didn't exist. It meant I had to work out a way to understand life, and for me, it was realizing that instead of being angry that she was taken away so soon, I became overjoyed that I had ever been loved by her at all.

He has embraced the idea that death means 'total nothingness' and is driven by the idea that we need to make the most of the short time that we have, to celebrate life.

I decided to ask my friend John, who grew up in a Christian family but isn't himself a Christian, about his experience after his mum died when he was a child.

> Growing up in a family full of faith, as someone without, means that you are very often living with contradictions. Without meaning to be crude, the 'rational' part of my brain says that I don't believe in God, meaning I don't believe in [an] afterlife, I don't believe in a pre-ordained 'purpose' to life and I don't believe in a reason why bad things happen. But it is very hard to dislodge the idea that God does exist, [and] that there is a purpose to life, if it's been taught to you from a very young age.

The result sometimes feels like you have a very deep anger towards a God that you don't, on another level, believe exists. Sometimes it feels that you exist in a sort of limbo between out-and-out atheism and faith, so you have a lot of misplaced anger. I don't believe in God, yet I am very angry at him. If I don't believe in God, who is at fault?

John described how grief was 'inevitably a different experience' for those who had a faith.

I have had conversations with family members along the lines of 'Well, I just know that we will see mum again,' which isn't any comfort to me. I simply don't believe it, and affirmation from someone who is sure of it doesn't make me feel any better, to be honest.

I still don't know how to process what happened. I do envy those with faith – knowing that it isn't necessarily easier for them – as to me, it seems that it must offer some sense of purpose. Even if they can't rationalize why bad things happens in this life, they do believe that things will be made good in the next life. I think without that belief everything does seem unjust.

But I don't feel a great sense of distance between my family and myself, and I think that comes down to the extent to which those people don't force things.

My advice to those of faith, with family members who aren't of faith, is to not force anything. It just makes things worse! I personally still feel quite angry when I go into churches, simply as a result of all the messages that are hung on the wall about the 'love of God'. It just feels like someone taking the piss when you have had something awful happen to you without any explanation.

But I think that if you have people of faith in your family who genuinely understand your frustrations, and actually admit to their own doubts, it does go a very long way to not creating any sense of divide.

Sacred Journeys

Even when I've felt distant from God, there has never been a time when I've really stopped thinking about all the questions that my mum's death provoked.

I recently watched *Extremely Loud & Incredibly Close*, a story about a nine-year-old boy, Oskar Schell, whose father died in the 9/11 attack on the Twin Towers in New York City. Most of the film is taken up by Oskar's obsessive search for a lock that fits the key he discovers among his Dad's possessions – an adventure that he, and we, assume he has undertaken alone. He accuses his mum of being absent – either asleep or forgetful. But in fact, it turns out that she has been going to every one of his search destinations beforehand, making sure it's safe and preparing the way for him. Afterwards, I wondered if this is what God is like. We may decide to strike out alone in search of answers, but whether we know it or not, he supports our quest, going ahead of us, full of love and concern.

When I look back on my life, I can see signs of this concern. It's what Marilyn McCord Adams calls 'the omnipresent tender loving care of God'. She compared God to an artist painting the story of our lives, someone able to work the horrific, ugly elements into a bigger canvas in which we will eventually be able to see his goodness to us. Listening to the stories that I've gathered together in this book has brought Marilyn's words to life for me. It wasn't that anyone denied the awfulness of what had happened to them. But in so many cases, they were able to look back and tell me about the ways in which God had been real to them at the time, had drawn close to them. 'Right at the heart of everything is this God who brings good out of bad, just as he brought resurrection out of crucifixion,' John Inge, who lost both his parents by the age of 13, told me.

I think I agree with the description of life used by the American writer Frederick Buechner in his memoir *The Sacred Journey*. Life is a journey in which he has experienced 'the compelling sense of an unseen giver and series of hidden gifts'. My prayer for you is that, one day, you are able to look back and find some of them, too.

Dan's Story

Dan was 19 and studying theology at Oxford when his brother, Mark, took his own life. They were very different people, even as children, Dan recalled, when we met up to talk about what had happened: 'Everything had gone right for me; people looked after me; I had made all the right decisions.' Meanwhile, Mark had suffered 'a litany of tragedies from a very early age', Dan said. After being caught up in their parents' divorce, Mark had become drawn to alcohol and to drugs. He had also been abused. At the time of his death, Mark was hearing voices all the time, had terrible visions and was making decisions which would put him into dangerous situations.

It was while Dan was in France in the summer holidays that he received a call from his father telling him that Mark had taken his own life. It was the first time that he had heard his father in tears. 'I remember sitting on the Eurostar just feeling that the whole world had fallen apart,' Dan told me. He felt numb, 'Like I hadn't slept for days', and exhausted. After initially breaking down into tears, he was then unable to cry and felt 'oddly stoic' about what had happened. It was in the autumn, as darker days drew in, that things began to fall apart.

Mark's death came at a time when 'everything was massively jumbled' for Dan. He was a gay man attending a theological college, questioning the faith of his teenage years and starting to reconstruct it. One of the most difficult things was dealing with some of the 'facile' things that people said to him. He can remember storming out of a church where the worship songs were all about 'how wonderful God was', while he was full of rage towards God. 'There was no space for that [anger]. I was feeling trapped by all this smiling Christianity,' he recalled. Being able to slam a door at his college, he said, was 'very helpful'.

Other things that helped him were saying morning and evening prayers every day. 'My life had been chaotic, my family was chaotic and I needed to learn how to look after myself with good routines and self-care,' he told me. A helpful chaplain described how, in the wake of a trauma, our idea of Jesus could be left like 'a shattered piece of stained glass on the floor and you've got to slowly piece it back together'. Going to cathedral services also helped. Even though for many months Dan felt 'absolutely nothing', he felt 'carried' by the service and by the enormous building; cathedrals have been described by some as 'ships of heaven'. He also remembers someone suggesting that he spend some time thinking about how Jesus draws near to people like his brother Mark. Dan recalled:

> What I did not want was people telling me what had happened to my brother, or what I should feel or who God was. I could only discover those things. That was the stuff that enraged me . . . Those who [actually] communicated Christ to me were those who stuck by and didn't give trite words, but who knew when to give me a hug without saying anything. They were really special moments.

Even today, Dan feels 'a deep sense of regret' about what happened to his brother. 'It's one of those things with suicide that everyone feels responsible but no one's responsible,' he told me. 'I think we all struggle with enormous guilt and shame and massive anger.'

If he could go back in time, Dan would tell himself to 'stick close to those good friends who love you' and reassure himself that 'the confusion and the darkness is not to be afraid of. Waiting is an important thing – waiting and trusting.' Today, he feels 'able to sit in the darkness with people and not be afraid of the darkness', knowing that 'out of all this horror God can still bring beauty, new possibilities and hope.' He also recommends reading the Psalms. One of his favourites is Psalm 27 which ends with: 'I remain confident of this: I will see the goodness of the Lord in the land of the living.'

CHAPTER 9
LOSING A SPECIAL PERSON
(& NADINE'S STORY)

My family are like four stretched elastic bands about to be pinged
and land so far apart that we never find each other again.
Something has to give. Someone in our house
has to say something.
Renée in *Paper Aeroplanes* by Dawn O'Porter

Ordinary People, a film that came out in the 1980s, tells the story of
a family dealing with the death of the eldest son, Bucky, in a sailing accident. In one scene, the surviving son, Conrad, startles his
mum while she's in Bucky's room, which hasn't been touched since
his death. Instead of talking about Bucky, they have a stilted conversation about golf and the weather.

Despite sharing a home, each person in this story is isolated. The
mother is desperate to carry on as normal and is embarrassed by
Conrad's mental health problems. Conrad is tormented by memories of the accident and convinced that he is somehow to blame. And
in the middle is the father, who is trying to mediate between the two
while privately mourning the loss of his other son.

Watching it recently, I thought about how, when death takes
someone away, the shape of your family changes. The complex web
that has taken years to build is cut, and the task of weaving it back
into a new one, in which everyone feels safe and included, can feel
impossible. Things will never be the same, and the 'new normal'

that people talk about might not be a threshold you want to cross. Simple questions like 'Do you have brothers and sisters?' or 'What does your Dad do?' can be ones you start to anticipate and dread.

In his brilliant poem, *Grief is the Thing with Feathers*, Max Porter writes:

> We guessed
> and understood that this was a new life
> and Dad was a different type of Dad now
> and we were different boys, we were brave
> new boys without a Mum

Grief can pull families closer. Sam described how, after their mother died, he and his sister developed a special connection:

> I had a strong sense of the two of us being in a kind of jolly-boat leaving the sinking ship and heading for the island. That was a bond between us . . . I think orphaned children, often siblings, can develop an extremely close relationship that it's difficult for anybody else to break into.

Looking back, I see me, my siblings and my dad as co-survivors of a shipwreck. Our memories of the storm may be different, but we all endured it. I also know, however, that death can place an enormous strain on a family. In *Intimate Loneliness*, a book about Gordon Riches' and Pam Dawson's work supporting bereaved parents and siblings, they describe how common it is for family members to feel 'surprise, hurt or exasperation' towards one another 'because they appeared not to be sharing the particular sort of pain that they themselves were feeling.'

Perhaps as you're reading this, you're feeling that you're drifting apart from those you share a home with. Or perhaps conversations in your family feel impossible to start. This is the case for Renée in Dawn O'Porter's novel, *Paper Aeroplanes*, who is living with her grandparents after the death of her mother. One day, Renée overhears her younger sister, Nell, crying in the toilets at school. 'How have we got to the point as a family where Nell is so full of pain that she sobs by herself at school, and I don't have the guts to knock on the door and ask her if she is OK?' she asks herself. Her grandparents have made it clear to her that talking about her mum is off-limits; it's simply too painful for them to contemplate.

If you find yourself in a similar situation, remember that there are people you can talk to outside your family, and that relationships change over time. I've sometimes found it's helpful to start a conversation with 'I', rather than 'you', which can make people feel defensive. 'I am really missing Dad' can be easier to hear than 'You never talk about Dad.'

Losing a Parent

My mum left an enormous hole in our lives when she died. When we did something celebratory, particularly at birthdays or Christmas, I would imagine an onlooker peering through the window, observing our brave attempts to be happy and normal, and I wondered whether they would be convinced by our performance.

For the first few weeks, my brother, sister and I went to stay with one of my mum's best friends. My dad was overwhelmed by grief and severely depressed, and I worried that he might take his own life. Even after we returned home and he went back to work, he was in an unstable place, desperately trying to find where God was in everything that had happened to us. His own dad had died when he was just a baby, and on top of his grief about my mum, all sorts of feelings about that had been stirred up – things he had never felt about such an early loss, the dad he had no conscious memories of whatsoever.

In so many ways, my dad was – and continues to be – a brilliant father. I never doubted that he loved us more than anything, and I'll always be grateful that he showed us it was okay to be sad, that he filled our house with photos of my mum and that there was never anything I felt I couldn't tell him. I know that he did his best. My mum's friends were deeply caring, and I will always be grateful to them, too. But I often felt that I was the only one monitoring what was happening to our family, alive to the potential for further things to go wrong at a time when we were so vulnerable. Some of my worries were probably irrational but others were not, and for many years afterwards I had a recurring dream in which I was desperately trying to warn everyone around me of a real, imminent danger, but nobody would listen to me.

When I spoke to Isobel Bremner at St Christopher's Hospice, she told me that after losing a parent, 'The biggest worry that most teenagers have is the other parent – that [fact] is just not said enough.' While her job is supporting children and young people, it's actually getting help for their parents that can make the biggest difference. It's like the instructions adults are given when they board a flight: in case of emergency, put on your own oxygen mask first, before you try to help your kids.

Although her words brought up difficult memories for me, I also found it reassuring to hear that other people had felt similarly to me. It really is frightening when you start to realize that your parents aren't superhuman, that perhaps they need help too.

Looking back, I was a bit like the 'mini-mothers and their instant kids' that Hope Edelman talks about in her book *Motherless Daughters*. Taking on things that my mum had once done made me feel close to her and proud of what I was managing to do. It was also a very handy distraction from my grief – I worked out that if I added these chores to my hours of homework, there was very little space left for sad feelings. It was also an effort to be in control at a time when the world appeared to be full of death and danger; I was convinced that my siblings needed my protection.

One of Hope's messages is that, in reality, it's not possible to replace a parent who has died. We want to be able to control our siblings, but we can't, and trying often only leads to conflict. It's the reason why, rather than bringing us closer, my attempts to mother my sister often simply led to rows. If I think of Sam's picture of the boat, I can see that I was constantly trying to grab the oars, even though I didn't really know how to row or know where we were going.

If you're worried about whether your parent is coping, remember that telling someone about this doesn't make you disloyal, and it doesn't mean that your family is failing. I like to remember the ending of *About a Boy*, Nick Hornby's novel that was later made into a film, in which Marcus, whose mum suffers from severe depression, has the realization that 'Two people isn't enough. You need a backup. If you're only two people, and someone drops off the edge, then you're on your own.' I think I'd expand this further: we often need more people than those in our immediate family.

Losing a Sibling

Amy Tan, an American writer, was 15 when both her father and older brother died of brain tumours within a six-month period. Her brilliant memoir, *Where the Past Begins*, tells the story of how, in the year in which those other family members were both dying, she and her younger brother were 'largely invisible' to their parents.

It was later, as an adult, that she looked through her father's letters and found that he had written about her being 'rebellious' during these months. A minister at the local church, he had worried about whether he had failed as a parent and as a Christian.

She wrote, in defence of herself as a teenager:

I could not bear what was happening and I had to withdraw. He should have understood that no fifteen-year-old should have to see death approaching every day. If he had failed me, it was because he saw me through the eyes of a minister who had had no time to make an appointment to see me. He had forgotten how to be a father. I did not want him to show me the sacrificial love of Jesus Christ or the beliefs he found in scripture. I wanted his love, the one that had once protected me and scooped me up after I had fallen.

Amy goes on to describe the many ways in which her father was great, but her experience of invisibility isn't unusual. Riches' and Dawson's research found that bereaved siblings of all ages described feeling 'left out, ignored and isolated within the family.' They also spoke about feeling protective towards their parents, but frustrated with them too, 'for their emotional fragility and tendency to exclude them'. One study found that, even years after a death, young people avoided talking about their sibling to their parents because they were so afraid of upsetting them.

Losing a child can put a huge strain on a marriage, creating further uncertainty for siblings. It's important to remember that you're not responsible for your parents' relationship, and to know that just because marriages are tested, that doesn't mean they always collapse. It really is possible for people to find their way back towards one another. It's also important to try to be generous when you're judging your family and to acknowledge small victories.

Have you managed to share a good memory of the person who died? Or spend an afternoon together without anyone storming out? Sometimes we need to celebrate these things.

Who Am I Now?

Our siblings shape who we are, and our relationships with them are often the longest of our lives. Losing a brother or sister can mean losing an ally, sparring partner, rival or protector. Some people grieving a sibling have described feeling purposeless, or struggling to make plans or decisions, wondering, 'What's the point?' It can leave you with questions about who you are now. Without them, what might your new role be? You can never replace them, but you may find that you are suddenly the focus of your parents' attention. You may feel pressure to fulfil their hopes, to make them happy. Other people might have said unhelpful things about you being their reason to go on.

In *Still Walking*, a beautiful Japanese film, Ryota feels he is always being compared unfavourably to his older brother, Junpei, a doctor (like their father) who died while saving a drowning child. Frustrated by his parents' tales about Junpei, he exclaims at one point: 'Who knows how Junpei would've turned out if he were still alive? We're only human.'

Ryota doesn't want to be a doctor and although his dad takes little interest in his chosen profession as an art restorer, he confidently pursues it, determined to carve out his own path through life. He will always be Junpei's brother, but he's also Ryota – an individual with a different set of dreams. As Molly put it so brilliantly in her story, remaining close to a sibling by remembering and celebrating them does not mean being a 'clone'.

Grief Is Grief

When I talked to Malcolm Guite, the priest-poet who works with students, about grief, he described how one young woman hadn't confided in anyone about the loss of her grandmother, who had looked after her when her parents were splitting up. 'I think she felt ashamed, or that other people wouldn't understand how close her grandmother had been to her, and that they would think she was making a fuss because it's not like losing a parent,' he explained.

But from her point of view, it felt as bad as losing a parent, if not worse . . . It doesn't matter whether it's a father or grandmother – if there's somebody who's been a really key part of your life who's not there anymore, it's like losing part of yourself.

Grandparents can be the people we confide in when things are tough at home. They are often the ones who believe the best of us, delighting in every one of our achievements and boasting about them to friends. They are repositories of brilliant stories; the family archivists who can connect us to our past. The death of a grandparent is often the first death that we grieve. It can be frightening to watch someone grow weak or frail, or to see your parents grieving for the loss of their mum or dad, realizing that they are someone's baby, just as you are theirs.

Alex, who lost his grandmother when he was 18, told me that his advice would be 'Don't be surprised if it affects you deeply.' He was very close to his grandparents, who had looked after him and his sister when they were little while their parents were working, and again later, for longer periods of time while his dad was being treated for cancer. 'They were more like second parents than grandparents,' he recalled. He remembers his granny as a source of stability and practical care – from the phone calls she would make to him to the cards she would send with newspaper cuttings and cartoons attached. Her sudden death, from undiagnosed spinal cancer, hit him hard at a time when things were already tough, and for a time, he struggled with depression. It left him wondering who the 'anchor' in his family would be now.

A Friend Is Gone

It's scary to confront the fact that people your own age can, and do, die. Caroline, who was 17 when her friend Jen died suddenly, remembers how 'surreal' it felt. 'The bounds of what you think is normal and possible are just completely rocked.' She can recall feeling 'completely disorientated' at school.

If you've lost a friend, you might be able to identify with the difficulties that Caroline encountered in communicating 'how big of a deal it was' to people who didn't know Jen. 'It was quite an isolating experience because it was this huge, life-altering thing that people didn't really relate to,' she told me. She remembers that some people were 'callous'. It's only now, years on, that she is able to appreciate that at this age, many people simply aren't familiar with grief: 'We hadn't practised doing all of this before.' What she recalls is the 'raw, awful pain' she felt and the 'utter emotional weight of having to process grief'. Crying at school was 'quite an embarrassing thing' that left her feeling vulnerable. 'I couldn't hold my cards close to my chest,' she said, but it wasn't something she could control. Small things such as one of Jen's favourite songs could trigger these tears, and it took Caroline a long time to be able to hear them with gladness rather than pain.

Looking back, she sees that one of the hardest lessons to learn was that when it came to supporting Jen's sister, simply being present would have been better than 'trying to frantically make it okay' – a hard lesson to learn when you're used to being a 'fixer'.

It's also important to acknowledge that you may be one of the people reading this who had a rocky relationship with a friend who has died. Perhaps what stands out in your memory are the times that you fell out or let one another down. There may be unresolved hurts or anger.

When I picked up Jacqueline Wilson's *Vicky Angel*, I imagined that it would be the story of a grieving for a perfect friend. In fact, Vicky is revealed to be a domineering presence in her friend Jade's life, and this doesn't change after Vicky dies suddenly – she reappears as a ghost who becomes increasingly controlling and bullying, and who guilt-trips Jade into decisions she doesn't want to make, preventing her from making new friendships. Several weeks pass before Jade is able to admit to a counsellor that there are things she *doesn't* miss about her friend. She has to practise standing up to Vicky, even after her death. Although it's a book aimed at younger readers, it's a reminder that it's okay to be honest with ourselves about the dark, as well as the light, sides of our relationship with the friend we have lost.

'You'd have liked him. You'd have liked her.'

The people I spoke to while writing this book liked telling me about the people they had lost. Not how they died, but what they were like. I got the impression that for some, it was the first time in a while that they had been asked to talk about the person.

This made me think about one of my favourite novels, *The Catcher in the Rye*, in which the narrator, 16-year-old Holden Caulfield, describes smashing all the windows of the garage the night his younger brother, Allie, dies of leukaemia. 'You'd have liked him,' Holden tells the reader. 'God, he was a nice kid, though. He used to laugh so hard at something he thought of at the dinner table that he just about fell off his chair.'

I love this passage because it reminds me that, sometimes, what we really want to talk about is how much we loved the person who has died, and to introduce them to more people – to make sure that others know all the things that made them so special. One of the nicest things my husband ever said to me when we first started dating was: 'Tell me about your mum.' Whoever it is you're grieving for, in Chapters 11 and 12 we'll look more at how we can remember them and carry them with us into our futures.

Nadine's Story

For Nadine, whose brother Steven was diagnosed with leukaemia when she was 14 and he was 11, all she wanted was to be 'normal'. 'I had just started high school,' she told me:

I really had my own life to lead. I was trying to establish myself in a new friend group. This whole thing was going to blow that all apart. So you had a choice: you could either become involved in it, or you could sort of hope it was going to go away.

The fact that her mother was searching for a cure for Steven gave Nadine the idea that maybe everything would be okay. But she also became the person that her mother confided in, sometimes with disturbing medical detail. 'I would sit and listen to her and I would be sympathetic and take it all in, but on the other hand I was a teenager and really didn't want this in my life,' she told me. 'Could somebody please take this away? Or maybe I could just half listen to it?' The possibility of talking about ordinary things seemed to be fading away.

With her father out at work and her mother spending a lot of time at the hospital with Steven, the whole dynamic of Nadine's home changed. 'Every time Mommy came home she was sad, and you never asked her about it,' she recalled. Although she had been told that Steven had 18 months to live – information that she pushed out of her thoughts – he died after just nine. Nadine was never told that things were getting progressively worse, and her parents had decided not to tell her other brother, who was nine at the time and very close to Steven, so the news came as a 'complete thunderbolt' to him.

Nadine's story is an example of the long-term impact that the wrong words can have. In her case, it was a teacher at her school who told her and her younger brother: 'God has left you behind, because you still have something you've got to accomplish. But he has taken Steven.' It sounded 'deliberate,' Nadine recalls. 'Steven was the chosen one by God, and I just wasn't up to scratch . . . I just remember that, up 'til then, I had sort of coped, and then I was told I wasn't good enough.' She wondered whether she had been left behind because wanting to be independent – to not participate in Steven's illness and death – was 'selfish and greedy'. She didn't know that this is in fact a very normal reaction for someone her age.

After Steven's death, things at home changed 'horribly', she said, with both of her parents blaming each other, and then themselves, for what had happened. Nadine felt under pressure to 'be good', to work hard at school and 'not rock the boat'. She remembers thinking 'The more invisible you can become, the better.' Her starkest memory is of Christmas Day that same year, which the family spent in the cinema, in the dark, where she could hear her mother crying. Steven's things were left untouched in the room that he had shared with his younger brother, which became 'like a shrine'.

For two years afterwards, her mother would go to the cemetery every day, where she would sit by Steven's grave and talk to him for hours. It caused arguments with Nadine's father who eventually decided to sell their house and move the family to a new home hundreds of miles away. Nadine, who was now at university, suddenly found out that her address had changed and that all of her possessions had been disposed of.

Nadine remembers that everyone in the family was sent to see a psychiatrist. Really, she just wanted to speak to her parents, but they were 'the last people you could talk to'.

'I would have liked somebody to say "It's alright for you to just get on with your life . . . There shouldn't be a set time for grief,"' she told me. 'Grief comes on different days of the week, it comes at different times of year, it comes in all sorts of different forms. I don't think people should be compelled into grief.'

Today, she still has nice memories of Steven, such as the way that he and her other brother would burst into giggles in the back of the car. The memory of that bleak Christmas in the cinema means that holidays are now very important to her, as is her belief in heaven. Despite her feelings of unworthiness, she has achieved an enormous amount in life in her profession as a lawyer. She can trace her approach to her work back to what happened to her, she thinks. 'I tell clients, "I'll always tell you the truth." I have to be able to leave their case feeling that I have done everything I could and don't have any regrets.' She is also 'more prone to crying and showing my emotion', she says. 'Being alive is being emotional, to me.'

CHAPTER 10
HOW IT FEELS
(& JERRY'S STORY)

I want this sadness that's been part of me since she died to go away.
It's like this mean little animal deep inside me. Munching at my guts.
Feeding on me day after day after day after day. Once in a while
taking a great vicious chomp. It hurts so much sometimes,
it's just about more than I can take.

Pam in *Alone at Ninety Foot*
by Katherine Holubitsky

One of the reasons I wanted to write this book was to offer reassurance to anyone worried that their response to death, their grief, was
not 'normal'. Isobel Bremner at St Christopher's Hospice has found
that young people who come to see her are often 'intensely critical' of
themselves. They believe that they are not doing grief 'right' and are
worried that they are 'uncaring, unloving or pathetic'. They need to
be reassured that however they are responding is okay.

Grief is hard enough without putting it under the microscope for
scrutiny. In this chapter, we'll look at some of the emotions that can
arise. What you read isn't a list of what's 'normal', but perhaps something here will reassure you that others have felt what you're feeling
and survived it.

Anxiety

My biggest struggle after my mum died was anxiety. Worries rotated
round and round in my mind like a carousel, and as soon as one

was dealt with, my mind would immediately slot in another one to fill the gap. I would read the Bible verse about giving Jesus my worries and think, '*I can't.*' My anxiety revolved particularly around my health. Although it was cancer that had led to my mum's death, my fears were attached to HIV/AIDs. I became obsessed with the idea that I must be extremely careful not to catch it, and I developed compulsive behaviours around washing my hands and checking with my dad whether he thought I had been infected. Although I understood the facts of the disease, I still worried that I could get it from simple everyday actions like shaking a person's hand and using bathrooms (if this is a specific fear for you, too, you might want to read *The Man Who Couldn't Stop* by David Adam, which reassured me that I wasn't alone).

Over the years, I worried about other diseases, too, but it was a long time before I was diagnosed with health anxiety. In my mid-20s I did a number of cognitive behavioural therapy (CBT) sessions – something that might be recommended to you if you have anxiety. It's a very practical form of therapy where the aim is to look at the connection between your thoughts and beliefs, and how you feel and behave. In my case, my therapist and I did a lot of calculations. As well as measuring the likelihood of something happening and how awful it would be (which meant saying my deepest fears out loud), I had to think about what I would do if it did happen, and the ways in which I would cope – I had to try to introduce some balance into my brain.

Finally, I had to make a list of what I really wanted to happen, instead of what I feared would happen. It made me realize that, in my heart, I tended to imagine a very bleak future. This isn't uncommon. Researchers have found that people who experience a traumatic event at a young age can develop a belief that things will turn out badly for them, or even that they will die young. Sometimes, like in my case, you have to work really hard to imagine an alternative.

Although I still struggle with anxiety today, I have found that simply recognizing it is helpful. I can tell myself 'What I'm feeling is anxiety,' and remind myself that there is often a big gap between what my mind is telling me and what is actually true. Something else I've found effective is doing very a simple breathing exercise: I breathe in through my nose for five seconds, hold my breath for a few seconds and then breath out through my mouth for five seconds. If you want, you can even get someone to count with you. Another technique is to put a boundary around your anxiety by setting aside a time every day – around 15 to 30 minutes – when you are allowed to worry. You can use this time to write down worries and, next to them, possible solutions. You might even find yourself struggling to fill the time.

Anger

Sometimes our anger has an obvious target: the driver who caused an accident or the doctor who failed to spot an illness. Sometimes we send it shooting off into our immediate surroundings. After my mum died, I remember seething when a family friend told me that they were going to plant a tree in memory of her – somehow it seemed outrageous that anyone would think that a *tree* could make me feel better.

It's also possible to be angry at the person who has died. In the film *Ordinary People*, Conrad, who survives the sailing accident in which his brother dies, is finally able to admit that he's angry with his brother for taking too many risks, for not turning back once the weather became dangerous. Even if the person was in no way to blame for what happened, you might feel angry with them for leaving you, or causing so much pain and throwing your family into chaos. Some people feel angry that they've been denied the opportunity to have a 'normal' adolescence, or are worried that they are missing out on things that their peers take for granted. Isn't this supposed to be the best time of your life?

Often, there is no obvious place for the anger to go. It's rage at the universe, that it should even be possible for this awful thing to have happened. Malcolm Guite, the priest-poet, told me that after the death of a student at his college, he was 'on the receiving end of, if you like, [a] kind of hatemail to God'.

'I regarded that as a very proper thing,' he added. 'A lot of people who have only a nodding acquaintance with the Church, with the Bible, don't realize that it's okay to be angry with God.' He points to the 'bitter and angry' Psalms. 'We have to license that voice because if the anger doesn't go out, it goes in and does damage.'

Drawing or other forms of art can be a good way of processing anger, as can physical exercise, and listening to music. I used to live by a river and when I felt overwhelmed by intense feelings, I'd go running. One of my favourite tracks was 'Death' by White Lies. The singer is taking off in a plane and admits that he's anxious: 'So frightened of dying . . . This fear's got a hold on me.' Although the words are bleak, the music is full of a soaring energy. The guitarist who wrote the lyrics, Charles Cave, once said that he hoped they might reassure people that 'It's alright to think and worry about these things.' It turns out that he's been a worrier since the age of seven.

Conflict

A normal part of moving into adulthood is establishing more distance between yourself and your parents – 'spreading your wings' and attaching more importance to relationships outside home. Privacy suddenly feels much more important, and it's normal to argue more with your parents, and to feel angry and resentful towards them. This doesn't necessarily change because grief has invaded your home.

When Professor Grace Christ worked with families in which a parent was dying of cancer, she found that, for those with sons and daughters aged 12 to 14, there was often a tension between their desire to spend time outside the family, or alone, and the family's need for emotional closeness. Parents often complained that they had no idea what their kids were thinking. Some of them were surprised that their sons or daughters wanted to carry on as normal or to grieve alone, behind a bedroom door. They couldn't understand comments like 'I'm fine' or 'Crying doesn't help,' or their children's determination to get on with life. Why didn't they want to share their feelings or to grieve together? Why were they so self-centred? Perhaps unsurprisingly, this could lead to arguments.

Professor Christ's advice is that parents shouldn't see a return to normal activities as 'callous indifference', but as an important part of growing up and 'a way of avoiding intense grief' until a person is able to confront their feelings more directly. If it helps, you could show your family this chapter, or even suggest that they look at Professor Christ's book, *Healing Children's Grief*, which contains lots of advice.

Sadness

Carrie, whose story we looked at earlier, told me that after her father died, she was convinced that she would never be happy again. She cried every week for two years. She found that putting a 'bracket' around her time alone in her grief was helpful:

I would set a timer every day for, let's say, 20 minutes and tell myself 'These 20 minutes or half an hour, I can cry or wail and let everything out, and when that timer is up, I am going to pick myself up and go outside and go for a run, or study or meet a friend, but it's going to end, it's not going to stay [like this] forever.'

For others, tears don't come. At St Christopher's Hospice, it's common for young people to be referred because they are not crying after being bereaved.

'I think that families put a lot of pressure on teenagers and children to talk and be articulate about themselves, and I don't think they necessarily have to be,' Isobel Bremner told me. Today, there's an emphasis on talking about our feelings, not bottling things up. But just because it isn't visible to others, doesn't mean that a person isn't grieving. Some people, for example, have to think through their grief, before they can feel it – they may need to spend time reflecting on what happened and why, how it's likely to affect their family, and what they need to do to get through it. For more expressive people, this can seem cold, but we need to remember that everyone is different. How we express or don't express our feelings is not a reflection of how much we loved the person who died. Nobody should feel coerced into outward displays of grief.

On the other hand, writers like the comedian Robert Webb have drawn attention to the fact that our willingness to talk, or show emotion, can be shaped by the messages we've received growing up. Rob's mother died when he was 17, and in his memoir, *How Not to Be a Boy*, he describes how being told to 'act like a man' can be like hearing that pain, guilt, grief, fear and anxiety are all 'unacceptable emotions for a man'. In fact, while today women tend to cry much more than men – at least in front of others – this is a relatively recent development. 'In the past, not only did men cry in public, but no one saw it as feminine or shameful,' writes Sandra Newman, an American writer in an essay 'Whatever happened to the noble art of the manly weep?' for the magazine *Aeon*. 'In fact, male weeping was regarded as normal in almost every part of the world for most of recorded history.'

Guilt

Goodbye Days, by Jeff Zentner, is the story of 17-year-old Carver Briggs who faces the prospect of a criminal investigation after his three best friends are killed in a car crash. The case centres on whether or not he knew when he sent a text that the friend receiving it was driving at the time, and that texting while driving is dangerous. The opening line is: 'Depending on who – sorry, whom – you ask, I may have killed my three best friends.'

'Am I certain that it was my text message that set into motion the chain of events that culminated in friends' deaths?' Carver asks. 'No. But I'm sure enough.'

His anxiety leads to panic attacks and, eventually, help from a psychiatrist, Dr Mendez, who gets him to tell different stories in which he isn't the cause of the accident. 'Our minds seek causality because it suggests an order to the universe that may not actually exist, even if you believe in some higher power,' Dr Mendez explains.

> Many people would prefer to accept an undue share of blame for a tragic event than concede that there's no order to things. Chaos is frightening. A capricious existence where bad things happen to good people for no discernible reason is frightening.

It's important to remember that feelings of guilt can arise even when we are clearly not to blame for something. Just because we have a strong feeling about something, that doesn't make it true. It's not unusual for people to blame themselves, rather than confront the terrifying reality that terrible things can happen randomly, in an unpredictable world. They may live expecting to be punished in some way for what happened.

Sometimes the guilt isn't about causing a death, but our feelings surrounding it. In Cathy Rentzenbrink's memoir, *The Last Act of Love*, she describes how tormented she was by the fact that, after several years of seeing her brother in a permanent vegetative state, she began to wish for him to die, not only for his sake, but for hers: 'I wanted to be free from worry about him.' Eight years after the accident that caused the condition, the judge agreed that the family could allow Matty to die. Although her brother was cremated, Cathy suffered from nightmares in which her brother was banging on the coffin lid from inside, or was chasing her, wanting her to join him in the grave. It took her many years to come to terms with what had happened. A turning point was doing research to understand her brother's condition and meeting doctors who were able to reassure her about her family's decision. She also learned to be kinder to herself – to acknowledge the terrible thing that had befallen her family, how hard she had worked to care for them, including her brother, and how normal her feelings were.

Talking . . . and Not Talking

Although most of the people I interviewed for this book had received counselling, not all of them had done it as a teenager – sometimes many years had passed first. You may have been offered it automatically or feel that friends and family are putting pressure on you to try it. You may be wondering whether to seek it out, or you may already be sitting on a waiting list.

When I asked Isobel Bremner how to tell when you need help, she gave a very straightforward answer: 'When you feel like you need help.' But there are also 'red flags' that you should pay attention to. If you are struggling with sleep or eating, finding it hard to get through the school day, using drugs or alcohol to numb or escape your feelings, isolating yourself (including dropping out of school) or self-harming, please do tell someone. If you ever think about taking your own life, it's vital that you tell someone. If you do decide to try a talking therapy, remember that there are lots of different types and that it's okay to look for one that works for you. And if, after a session or two, you feel that you don't 'click' with the person you are talking to, then you can always ask to see someone else.

I've had mixed experiences over the years. I remember feeling, when I was 11, that my counsellor would only be happy if I told her I was feeling unhappy, even if that day I was feeling okay. I don't like feeling pressured to accept a particular interpretation of my situation or how I feel, and I think the best experiences are with people who truly listen, even on days when you sit in the waiting room wondering if you can come up with anything to say at all.

Counselling can never reverse what has happened, but if you're curious about whether it could help to talk to someone in confidence, I do recommend trying it. Just having a dedicated period of time to be listened to by someone outside your immediate circle, whose only job is to help you find a way forward, without judging you, can be really helpful. Another option is to meet up with other people who have been bereaved. If there aren't any groups in your area, there are national charities who can help you get in touch with others online or in person.

Small Good Things

Amid all the advice and help I received after my mum died, one thing that stands out didn't come from a counsellor, doctor or teacher, but my 14-year-old best friend, Bex. 'Just put *The Simpsons* on and take a break from thinking about things,' she suggested. I felt guilty about following her advice at first – was I really allowed to stop worrying? But I was so exhausted at this point that I did. And it was like a little escape into a yellow world where nothing ever seemed to go too badly wrong.

I think of things like this as 'a small, good thing', which happens to be the title of a short story by the American writer, Raymond Carver, which tells the tale of a bereaved couple cared for by a baker who offers them 'warm and sweet' rolls. 'Eating is a small, good thing in a time like this,' he tells them.

You might want to come up with your own list of 'small, good things' – it could be looking after yourself by getting your hair cut, going for a run or swim, or watching a favourite TV series. Treat yourself as you would someone else in pain. Be kind to yourself.

Jerry's Story

When Jerry was eleven years old, the headmaster of his boarding school asked him to come to his office. Jerry assumed that he was going to be asked about a letter he had written to his parents, but instead he was told that they had been in a plane crash. Jerry recalled:

> They never used the words 'Your parents have died.' They said, 'Your parents have been involved in a terrible plane crash.' At that point I thought, 'I am meant to cry now,' and then I did start to cry, but I didn't actually know if they had died . . . All I was wanting to ask was, 'Had they died?' But I didn't know, and I didn't feel I could ask.

It was only later, while sitting in the back of his uncle's car driving away from the school that day that Jerry finally got the confirmation. Because of the political situation at the time, his parents' bodies were never returned to the UK. Jerry described how, in the years that followed, he 'kind of suppressed it all'. 'I cried a bit at the time, but I could never cry after that,' he recalled. 'I just totally shut off my emotions.'

He had had no particular interest in God before the plane crash, but at a memorial service for his parents something changed. 'I encountered God in a profound way,' he told me.

> I walked out of that service just knowing that God loved me, had a plan, [and] was going to create something good out of this. I can't even remember what was said from the front . . . I just encountered the Holy Spirit in a really deep way.

Jerry's faith was something that he kept private. Christians seemed 'a bit weird' to him and although he had a 'deep conviction it [what he experienced] was true', he didn't want 'any Churchy stuff that went with it'. Although he had lots of friends, he had no idea what he was doing in life and often felt quite lonely. When he was choosing what to study at school, where to go to university and what to do afterwards, he felt lost.

After university, he went travelling for a year and got into trouble a number of times in different places, occasionally asking God

'What am I doing?' before recovering and putting God aside again. At times, he felt afraid, but chose to ignore it: 'It was a weird combination. I took loads of risks and did risky things . . . I was like, "I'm not going to be wrapped up in fear."'

When he came home, he got very sick on a drug used to prevent malaria, which seemed to act like 'an atom bomb in my brain'. But even when talking to a counsellor, he found he wasn't ready to face what had happened to his parents. He was in his mid 20s before that time came – the turning point came one day at church, after he'd been prayed for, when he cried for the first time in 15 years.

Today, Jerry is married with two children of his own. Having once been unable to talk about what happened to his parents, he can do so easily today. In fact, a few years ago he gave a talk at a church, in which he shared the story of the crash. Incredibly, a man in the congregation, who was only in the country for a week and had almost not come to church at all, came up to him afterwards to say that his parents had been killed in the same crash.

When I asked Jerry to tell me his story, he told me that he wasn't sure how useful it would be because as a teenager, he had shut his feelings down so completely. But I think his story is important. Perhaps you've been told that you *must* talk about your feelings, but don't feel ready, or able, to do so. Perhaps you simply don't want to.

Jerry suggested to me that people should be invited to talk but not forced. And I agree. His story is a reminder that it can take years for us to do the hard work of grieving for somebody, and that tears can come many, many years after we first lose somebody. And even if we talk to nobody else, God is with us. Not everybody might have the amazing experience that Jerry had at that memorial service, but what he learned – that God is with us, supporting us and is on our side – is as true for you as it was, and is, for Jerry.

'It's a scar not an open wound now,' he told me. 'That's the difference.'

CHAPTER 11
THE ART OF
REMEMBERING
(& WILL'S STORY)

*They're not just clothes, Dad, they're what's left over
after a beautiful life has ended. Just like the photos and videos,
these are a handle on the best person any of us ever knew.
There's no such thing as just clothes, just perfume, just ornaments,
not when they've been touched by somebody's life, by Mum.*
John, in *The Lost Boys' Appreciation Society*
by Alan Gibbons

It's now over 20 years since my mum died, but I think about her at least once a day. I can bring to mind general things: the shape of her face, the tanned skin on her back in summer, the way she said my name. And I can remember specific moments in time, like the instructions she gave me after sewing me into a 101 Dalmatians outfit for a party (which I subsequently forgot, rendering me unable to eat thanks to my paws). If somebody asked me to describe her, I could do it with ease. I wish I had known this as a teenager, when I was worried that my memories of her would fade.

Just Things

In my family, it was easy to talk about my mum after she died. We kept pictures of her all over the house, and for many years my parents' bedroom remained unchanged: her clothes hung on the same rails, her jewellery and perfume lay unused on her dressing table. It was many years before we began to put things away, and today I have a box containing things that I kept, including a thick, brightly coloured jacket, a recipe book that belonged to her mother and a diary that she kept the year before she died. Whenever I look at them, not only does my mum appear in my mind, but it feels like I'm being transported to another world: my childhood, before everything changed.

Before I left home at 18, I would sometimes feel anxious that leaving things as if my mum was still alive was morbid or unhealthy. In films the fact that someone has left a deceased person's room intact is usually a sign that something is wrong – that they are in denial about what has happened. I don't think that was the case for us, but maybe leaving the house unchanged was a sort of silent resistance against any suggestion that we 'move on', and obediently progress through the usual practical steps expected of grievers. We would do what we wanted, when we wanted.

I know that we didn't want to go to the other extreme, erasing any sign that my mum had existed. Perhaps that's why we kept my mum's clothes for so long – they seemed so intimate. She had picked them out, washed them, hung them up and matched them with jewellery and perfume. I knew that she would never need them again, but getting rid of them felt like saying that out loud.

I don't think that there is a single set of rules we can apply when it comes to possessions, but my personal tips are:

1 It is okay to keep some things. You can take your time when choosing. Think carefully about what you would like to keep and why, and find somewhere safe to keep it. I've come to see that doing this can be a better way of treasuring possessions than simply keeping everything. One idea is to create a memory box. A cardboard or plastic storage box is fine, but some people like to use one that belonged to the person or find one that they can decorate. I don't regularly look at my box, but it gives me enough comfort to know that these things are safe.

2 You don't have to do everything at once: you can pack away possessions, like clothes, for example, without giving them away, and perhaps do that at a later stage.

3 If you are going to be spending time sorting through things, make sure that you plan in activities that offer you a break: a trip to a film or a chat over the phone with a friend. I have found that sorting is a tiring process, because possessions inevitably give rise to memories, and choosing what to keep and what to give away is emotionally tasking. Be gentle with yourself.

Remembering with Honesty

Over the years, I've thought about how we can remember someone in their entirety, in three dimensions. How do we cherish somebody without flattening their memory, without erasing their complexity? One of Frankie's frustrations in Sandra Chick's *I Never Told Her I Loved Her* is that she doesn't recognize the stories that her dad tells about her mum. Her memories are that her parents weren't happy together, but 'To listen to him now, you'd imagine their life together had been perfect.'

Perhaps the best thing we can do is to remember people the way we think about those around us: as individuals with strengths, flaws and quirks. Nobody is perfect – we are all capable of hurting others and getting things wrong. To say so isn't to disrespect them once they have died, but to say that we loved them as they really were.

Not everybody wants to embark on a journey of discovery about the person who has died – sometimes we are happy to cherish our own memories, rather than seek out other people's. But if you do want to learn more, it can be helpful, and fascinating, to speak to others who remember them, such as people they worked with, people who knew them before you were born.

Will, whose father died suddenly when he was four, told me that when he went to a reunion at the school where his dad had been a teacher, he'd had 'Loads of great conversations – "Your dad did this, your dad did that; He was a legend.'" Something that he found particularly comforting was hearing 'How much I am like him, in terms of personality, sense of humour, interests, hobbies, things like that.'

Special Places

After my mum was buried, it was many years before we arranged for a gravestone. Even though my dad has since designed a beautiful one that's in place, it's not somewhere I visit. My feeling is that my mum isn't there, but with God. But for some people, a grave or place where ashes are kept becomes an important place: somewhere to visit and remember.

Some churches and crematoriums hold services of remembrance. Andrew, the rector I asked about funerals, holds an annual service called 'In Loving Memory' around the date of All Souls – the day in November when Christians traditionally remember people who have died. Anyone who has lost someone in the past one to three years is invited to come along, and the church is often full. Each participant can light a candle and write the name of their loved one on a leaf, which is attached to a tree in the church. Families can also dedicate a rose bush in the churchyard to the person who has died.

Andrew believes that there is a 'huge demand for rituals for remembrance' in our communities. In the past, such rituals were far more common. Today, we associate Hallowe'en with dressing up and trick-or-treating, but the name actually means 'the eve of All Hallows' or the eve of All Saints Day (November 1st) – the day when Christians remember saints. It is followed by All Souls Day on November 2nd. I've never really liked Hallowe'en – I don't like to think about disembodied ghosts and ghouls. But I have grown to like the idea of the following two days – the opportunity to remember people, pray for them and affirm that they are safe with God. My Mexican friend, Juve, told me that at home they celebrate and remember their loved ones on November 2nd, too. They call it Día de los Muertos (Day of the Dead).

In my village, if someone passed away in the past year, when the Day of the Dead came around, you would make in a room or a space in your home an altar for them, and in that space you would provide them with the things that they used when they were alive . . . And usually there's a big picture of them with all the saints. Anyone that knew this person could just come into your home and either bring their own things to the shrine or just remember that person.

Juve added that the skulls painted with flowers and images of dancing skeletons that you see don't represent 'anything gruesome or bad. It basically means life. . . In a way, I think that's the whole point of the holiday: we are celebrating life.'

Writing this book, I loved hearing about the creative ways that people had found to remember the people they loved. Molly wears her sister Dom's clothes, and her parents have both got a tattoo identical to one that Dom had, in her handwriting. It reads *Amor Vincit Omnia*, which means 'Love conquers all'.

'Rituals really helped me,' Carrie told me.

[Like] writing letters to my dad. We used to like going on runs together, so I would go on runs and imagine I was doing it with my dad . . . Putting pictures up in the house and speaking to the picture. Doing rituals around Christmas or his birthday where we all shared a memory about him. Going out and buying a certain type of coffee that I knew he liked in honour of him . . . If you believe in an afterlife I think that can be a really sweet way to maintain your connection in the midst of loss.

In our interview, Joanna Collicutt told me that there was nothing necessarily wrong with having conversations with someone after their death and that it's not uncommon for people to have 'uncanny' experiences, like hearing the voice of the person. In her story, Meryl mentioned that she still occasionally talked to her dad – more than 50 years after his death when she was 19.

Grieving Online

The way that we remember is also evolving in the digital age. Reading this, you might be wondering about what to do with a person's social media sites after they die. It's possible to request that Facebook or Instagram take down someone's account, for example, but you can also ask that it become a memorial. In general, you won't be able to log in and change anything, but you may decide that it's a nice way to remember them. You might decide that you want to download some of your favourite pictures and put them in an album.

It's also worth thinking about your use of social media when you're grieving. For example, consider how much information you want to make public. Is what you're writing something that you want everybody to see, or should you share it with a smaller group of people or a trusted friend? Could you wait until the morning before writing it, just to check whether your feelings have changed? Like speaking in front of large crowds, sharing with large numbers of people can leave you feeling vulnerable and exposed afterwards. You could also consider changing your settings, so that only certain people can see certain posts or pictures.

Another thing to think about is how what you share might affect other people close to you, who are also grieving. It might be a good idea to discuss together what you all feel comfortable making public, so you at least know what is likely to cause upset. Some people are much more private than others, and it may cause a lot of pain if a picture or memory appears in their feed, with no warning. It could also be hard for them to learn via social media how you are really feeling, if at the moment you're finding it hard to be open with one another. Social media can be great, but it's no substitute for a face-to-face conversation with those closest to you. Maybe ask yourself whether you might be using it to avoid those conversations.

When it comes to your online interactions you had with the person who died, it's natural to want to preserve them. When my friend Heather's brother was killed suddenly in a hit-and-run, she realized that something she still had was all the WhatsApp messages from him. She was able to export the messages in two clicks:

> It was a sad process to read back and remember so many great conversations, which illustrated how wonderful he was. It was so important for me to have those because of what it demonstrated about his character, including my favourite, a note just to me that said, 'I would like to establish a regular communications cadence with you.' He was living on the West Coast of the USA at the time, and we were in London, so obviously eight hours apart doesn't happen if you aren't intentional about it.

In an article for the *Financial Times* ('How technology is changing the way we grieve', March 2018), Emma Jacobs described how she carried on texting her dad after he died. Another writer, Candi Cann, would regularly call her brother's mobile phone to listen to his voice, a year after his death. The nearest I have is a video of my mum, which we have since transferred onto a digital format to make sure we'll be able to watch it in future. Fortunately, as Heather found, there are lots of ways that digital content, including voicemails, can be saved for the future.

Vivid and Specific

After his dad died, Simon Bray set up the 'Loved and Lost' project where he gave people the opportunity to talk about someone who had died, and to recreate a favourite photo. Simon would return with them to the exact spot where they had been photographed with their loved one and take another, this time without them. Explaining the idea, he wrote: 'When grieving, people want to know that we're coping, but, really, what we want to talk about is the person who is gone.'

His interviews are beautiful because they really bring each person to life in vivid detail.

If you're worried that you might forget the person you love, I hope you'll be reassured to hear that the people I interviewed for this book still have strong memories of their parents and siblings, even decades after their deaths. In the early days, weeks and months of grief it can be hard to concentrate, and you might worry that your memories are hazy or hard to access, but that doesn't mean that, over time, that fog won't clear.

When you're ready, I hope that you'll find people to talk to about your own memories, that you'll be able to tell them all about the person you love: what made them unique, what made them laugh, what conversations you wish you could have with them today. Barney, Paul Fiddes' son, told me that it was hard when he started university because nobody knew his brother, Ben, who had died. 'It's always really nice to know that there are people out there who knew him really well that I could talk to if I wanted,' he said. 'That's a really nice thing – to try to continue seeing people who knew that person.'

Sometimes it's the specificity of memories that fills our hearts. I always enjoyed the scene in *Sleepless in Seattle* in which Tom Hanks, whose wife has recently died, tells his little son: 'She could peel an apple in one long, curly strip.' Perhaps you could make your own list of what made your person special. In Chapter 12, we'll explore how to take these memories with us forward into the future.

Will's Story

'I suppose I have experienced a lot more bereavement, by a relatively young age, than most people will have,' began Will, when I asked him to tell me his story.

Both of his parents died of heart disease 'very suddenly and completely unexpectedly'. His father had a heart attack in his sleep when Will was four, and when he was 13, his mother died after an aneurism (that's when a blood vessel swells beyond its normal size). Now in his early 20s (Will lived with foster families as a teenager and has finished university), he told me that his memories of his mother's death remain vivid:

I had been to church that morning, and my mother had been resting with a migraine. That was nothing unusual, so I thought very little of it. She seemed okay when I returned home, and she said she was just going to have a quick lie down before going to get the Sunday shopping . . . and the next thing, I just heard this massive crash in the room and that was my mother. At first I thought, 'This can't be happening. This is what you see on *Casualty* and *Holby City*,' and then it was, 'Gosh no, this is happening. I must dial 999 immediately.'

Will was full of praise for the medics who tried to save his mother – from the paramedics, to the doctors and nurses at the hospital, to the 'fantastic' hospital chaplain. The team spent an hour trying to resuscitate her before 'a man in a suit came along', he remembers:

He took me into the room and said, 'William, there is no easy way of saying this, but your mother's died. We are preparing the body, if you would like to see her in about 15 minutes,' and so I did, and I saw her in that room. She looked very peaceful. I was still trying to get my head around what had just happened, and I remember I held her hand, on the advice of the nurse, and I prayed there and then – that was my decision, to pray, and I then left the room 20 minutes later, and my last words to her were 'See you in heaven,' and I then closed the door.

He continued: 'As well as feeling upset, lost and empty in some ways at the time, I also started worrying. It was almost silly, really – I started worrying about practical things like "Oh gosh, how am I going to pay the bills?"' Will's questions were very normal – it's natural for our thoughts to spin at a time like this, occasionally towards urgent practical questions about who will look after us.

After leaving the hospital, Will lived with his godparents for six months before going into foster care. His life changed 'completely, but with lots of consistency', he recalled. Going to school after he'd been home-educated was also a big change, though he eventually really enjoyed it. Counselling also played a big part in Will's journey. He told me that, while he knew that his mother had died, 'It took me about six months for it to really emotionally sink in,' at which point it 'just hit me like a tonne of bricks'. Talking to a counsellor at school was 'incredibly helpful', he added. 'I would say I relied on the counselling for three years, but for the last two years of counselling it was more of a safety net. It was nice to have, but I did not really rely on it as such.'

Will is one of the few people I have met who lost both parents at such a young age, and I was very struck by how important his faith had been to him during such a traumatic time and how supportive the Church had been. 'I've always believed in God, in his existence,' he explained.

I would say that after I was orphaned at 13, that was when my belief and trust in God started to develop, and I started finding myself consciously praying more, subconsciously following the services more, because I realised my absolute dependence on God.

One of his favourite poems is *Footprints*.

It gets how God has always got us it, but it also gets that whole 'What can we see at the time; what can we see with hindsight?' distinction as well. It has become more apparent to me over time where God was in particular actions and particular events, than perhaps it was at the time.

When I asked Will if he had any advice for readers, he said, after a pause:

I think I would say, sometimes you do need time alone, but seeking company and being in company is very healthy. However much you are talking, however much you are not talking, just making sure that there is someone there if that's what you feel you need, immediately afterwards, particularly.

He was keen to get across that when we can't find the words, 'God already knows what is on our hearts.' Prayer, he said, is 'also about just being and listening for God, and letting God impart things to you'.

We ended our conversation by talking about remembering our parents. For Will, looking at photos is helpful, as well as visiting the grave where both of his parents are buried in Yorkshire. He remembers that, a few months before she died, his mother told him, 'If something happens to me, I don't want you looking back into the past all the time.'

'I know that she would want me to look to the future and focus on the present while, of course, acknowledging the past – to get a good balance of that,' he said.

Remembering my parents is very helpful for me. And I used to get upset, but I don't get upset doing it now. I find it very joyful to remember my parents, looking back on their lives with love and, ultimately, looking towards the future when we will be united again.

CHAPTER 12
WHAT DOES THE
FUTURE HOLD?

Moving on, as a concept, is for stupid people, because
any sensible person knows grief is a long-term
project. I refuse to rush. The pain that is thrust upon
us let no man slow or speed or fix.
Grief is the Thing with Feathers by Max Porter

It was Isobel Bremner at St Christopher's Hospice who taught me the phrase 'continuing bonds'. It's thanks to her that I decided not to call this chapter 'Moving On'. 'I don't use phrases like "letting go", "moving on", or "closure" because you don't move on do you?' she told me. 'Some of the language that is commonly used around grief is not especially helpful. I think it's about helping somebody to live with the death in the best possible way.'

In the past, grieving people were often specifically encouraged to 'move on', to separate themselves from the person who had died, leaving them behind in order to focus on the future. Understandably, this was often not what people wanted to hear (I remember initially struggling to talk about my mum in the past tense). Over time, those working with grieving people – psychologists and social workers – started to challenge this thinking.

Among them was Dr Phyllis Silverman, an American psychotherapist who co-authored a book called *Continuing Bonds*. She explained some of the ideas behind it in an article for *Psychology* magazine ('Thinking about continuing bonds', May 5, 2010):

A person does not always have to be present for us to feel connected. When the absence is the result of a death, it is necessary to change the nature of the relationship rather than letting it go. As in life, relationships change shape and form as time passes. They may live in our memory, in the things we do, in the stories we tell.

Dr Silverman did a lot of work with children and teenagers, and found that they naturally developed these bonds, with dreams being one of the ways in which they stayed connected to those who had died. Others sought out people who could tell them more about the person, or thought about how they could live in a way that would make the person proud.

When someone told Carrie that she didn't have to 'move on', it came as a huge relief. She felt:

> I don't have to keep clinging so hard to these memories because I'm afraid someone is going to take them from me, or time is going to take them from me. I can hold onto them for as long as I want in whatever way that I want.

A picture that I've found helpful is 'Growing Around Grief', something shared by the counsellor, Dr Lois Tonkin. She described how a person grieving drew a circle to represent herself and then coloured it in entirely with the shading representing her overwhelming grief. Because this person had been told that time was a healer, she expected her grief to become smaller and less all-consuming. What actually happened was that the grief remained the same, but that her life grew around it. This was represented by a much larger circle.

Dr Tonkin explained:

> When people experience a major loss, they often can't imagine how they can ever be happy again. But as time goes by, other

people and other experiences come into their life, and they find themselves taking pleasure in living again; not because they have 'forgotten' or 'got over' their loss, but because it has become part of who they are.

(It's important to say here that we don't *have* to have a continuing bond with someone who has died. Sometimes their death is a relief because their impact on our life was overwhelmingly negative. Relationships are complex. And even if we do maintain a bond, we will face the challenge of moving forward with our lives without their physical presence.)

New Starts

One of the things that I noticed when reading fiction about teenage grief was that most of the stories end with a hopeful scene. The main character turns some kind of corner and begins to face the future with a new sense of purpose. Their relationships with those around them start to thaw. For example, in *Alone at Ninety Foot*, Pam finally manages to have a long talk with her dad, about why her mum took her own life. As the book ends, she is preparing to 'live life and love life'. In Judy Blume's *Tiger Eyes*, in which Davey loses her father in a violent burglary, the story ends with her mum finding the strength to move them all back home, after months of living with relatives. 'Some changes happen deep down inside of you,' Davey observes. 'And the truth is, only you know about them.'

It made me wonder about what progress looks like in real life and how there isn't always a neat chapter ending. Some people have drawn up stages of grief, almost as if we could tick them off to ensure we are doing it properly. Yet the way we feel days, weeks, months and years after someone dies is not something we can necessarily control. You might have a few days when you surprise yourself by feeling strong and hopeful, only to be taken aback by feelings of intense sadness later that week. Worrying that we are not doing grief 'right' can make it all even worse. Should we still be feeling so distraught three years later? Or, on the other hand, can it be right that we are laughing just a week after the funeral?

In *The Last Act of Love*, her book about the death of her brother, Matty, Cathy Rentzenbrink has a list of things she feels guilty about:

I feel guilty about enjoying things
I feel guilty that I can't just enjoy things
I feel guilty for being happy
I feel guilty that I'm not happier . . .
I feel guilty that I can't just get over this
I feel guilty that I could ever get over this.

I hope that one of the messages you will take from this book is that grief isn't a test that you're required to pass. I hope that the stories included will help you to see that it's a different experience for everyone. Only you can do your journey through grief – it is not for anyone else to set deadlines or goals. When you grieve, you are doing one of the hardest things humans have to do in a lifetime, the thing that made Jesus himself weep and groan.

I like how Malcolm Guite puts it:

Grief is a big thing. It is as big, and as long, and [as] complicated as your life with somebody was. And just like you didn't have to do all of the getting to know and love the person all at once in a special, three-day crash course – you did it gradually – you have to do the same with grieving. Because it is like the other side of it. Grief is an expression of love.

Future You

If adolescence is full of endings – leaving childhood behind, finishing school, leaving home – it's also a time of beginnings. I remember the feelings of excitement and relief that bubbled up as I set off for university at age 18. Although I loved my dad and my siblings deeply, our house contained so many memories, not only of my mum's illness but of the difficulties of the subsequent years. Away from home, it was impossible to monitor what was happening there, so I gave myself permission to focus on my immediate surroundings and, to a certain extent, present myself afresh. At university, nobody knew anything about my life before I arrived, and there was something liberating about that.

Although studying English – my mum's subject – made me feel close to her, I didn't feel under pressure to follow in her footsteps or to meet any family expectations. My dad always made it clear that he only ever wanted me to be happy.

I know that this isn't the case for everyone. In her research, Professor Grace Christ found that people aged 15 to 17 who had lost a parent tended to be 'more concerned about becoming the person the parent wanted them to be, about living up to the parent's expectations' and that, at times, these expectations were 'overwhelming'.

Others may feel an internal pressure to excel. In his memoir, *How to Be a Boy*, the comedian Robert Webb describes how, after his mum died when he was 17, he decided that the way to give this awful event meaning was to turn it into a story in which he, the 'suffering hero', would conquer the world. His mum would 'sing' through his achievements.

Remember that this is your life and not anyone else's. Although it's good to receive affirmation that a lost parent or sibling would have been proud of you, it's for you to work out what is right for you. Your job isn't to make up for what happened or live a certain way because they weren't able to.

Forward and Back

Grief can resurface at different points in our lives. I remember bursting into tears when, at my 21st birthday, my dad pulled out a big brown envelope full of photographs from my childhood. Although

I had some counselling immediately after my mum died, I have been back several times since, and found it helpful to talk through memories and anxieties that have risen to the surface as I've got older. I remember one counsellor describing what had happened as a wound: we could open it up and try to clean it out, but it would always leave a scar.

You might also find that, over the years, other sorts of endings are more painful. A sibling moving out, the end of a relationship or the departure of a teacher you have been close to can all trigger memories of your bereavement. You might want to find ways to mark these endings, such as writing the person a letter or making a list of what you've learned from them.

It's hard to talk about the way grief shapes us positively without suggesting that there was some kind of silver lining to what happened; we need to be able to say that nothing could ever make it a 'good' thing in our lives. I think it's the same when it comes to the belief that God can bring good out of bad. As Malcolm Guite told me:

We can have a faith that out of all kinds of difficulties and darkness God can bring great life, but if we just rush to guessing wildly at what that great light might be, and thrusting onto somebody the duty of being thankful for something that hasn't even happened yet, we are complicit with the denial, really, that something terrible has happened.

Yet we know that grief does shape us. In his book on supporting children and teenagers who have experienced trauma, Dr Atle Dyregrov writes that we can gain a stronger understanding of what matters in life. He lists: 'increased intimacy with people they care about, a clearer experience of what is important and what is unimportant, or an increased sense of the intensity of being alive'. He also highlights: 'confidence in their ability to handle difficult situations, and knowledge about how they can help a friend who is having a hard time'.

I heard so many echoes of this in my interviews – from Sam describing how the experience of watching his mother die for such a long period of time had influenced his decision, many years later, to work in places where life was difficult; to Dan talking about his ability to 'sit in the darkness' with other people.

Isobel Bremner and her colleague, Patsy Way, believe that people like us often see the world from a 'unique and different standpoint' and discover qualities that we would not have found had we not had this experience. They have compared it to having a house with rooms you never knew existed:

> These rooms may initially be dark, but with some exploration they may discover gifts, strengths and sides to themselves they never knew existed. They can also, should they wish to, shut the doors of these rooms and return to ordinary adolescence.

As I said at the start of this book, I sometimes think that losing someone early in your life means joining a club that you never wanted to be part of. However much you learn from the experience, however much it shapes you, you would still rather it had never happened, that you had never needed to become stronger, wiser or more compassionate in the first place.

A new awareness of 'what matters' can sometimes be quite lonely. A death can make you ask enormous questions about life and your own purpose – questions that might never have occurred to the people around you. While losing my mum made me hold the people I love close, it has also removed a sense of safety I should have had for longer – I learned at age 12 that the world is a risky, uncertain place.

If I could travel back in time and talk to my teenage self, I think I would tell her that so many of the things she worried about didn't come to pass. But even today, I often find that moments of deep happiness are accompanied by an underlying hum of anxiety – 'Is this too good to be true? What if it's taken away?' I know that I have a tendency to let my mind wander along dark paths, worrying about future losses and my own mortality, but I also believe in the God my family and I sing about every Christmas in the small, candle-lit church in the village that's one along from the town I grew up in:

> Light and life to all he brings,
> Risen with healing in his wings.

Ultimately, I believe that this is our world's destination – not death and darkness but light and life. We were not made for a life narrowed by fear, but one lived with courage, in the knowledge that ultimately, God has conquered every darkness it contains. As Jesus tells us in the Book of John: 'I have come that they may have life, and have it to the full.' When the band White Lies describe the fear of falling from the sky in their song 'Death', they ask 'Could there be love beneath these wings?' We can answer, *yes*.

You Are Not Alone

As I reach the end of this book, I find myself looking back on all the stories I've heard from people offering lights for the path, and I wonder if I have done them justice. Writing each chapter has been harder than I thought it might be, sending me back to painful memories, and reminding me that there are still times when the path seems dark. But these stories have also helped me to see the truth of Dr Lois Tonkin's drawing of a circle: it is possible to grow around grief.

The loss of someone you love is a defining thing. But it will not be the only one. I think about Meryl walking around her beautiful house on the Suffolk marshes, full of the art she and her husband have created and collected, occasionally saying, 'Hey, how about that, Dad?' And about how Barney can see glimpses of his brother, Ben, in his two children. 'I have been able to talk more about Ben to them than I have [to others] for the last 20 years because I want them to know about him,' he told me. I also think about the ways in which people were able to look back and see signs of an 'unseen giver' in their lives.

I think about a picture of my mum standing on the doorstep of her little house in Liss on the morning of her wedding, beaming. She had lost her own mum as a teenager, but there she was, on the threshold of a new life with my dad, and before long, me.

I don't know where you find yourself now, on your path, or what might lie ahead for you, but my prayer is that you will know that you are not alone, and that light and life awaits you, even if it takes some time for the night to turn to day.

Further Reading and Sources of Help

Fiction and memoirs

Losing a father:
Tiger Eyes, Judy Blume (Macmillan)
The Sacred Journey, Frederick Buechner (Harper Collins)

Losing a mother:
The Lost Boys' Appreciation Society, Alan Gibbons (Orion)
Alone at Ninety Foot, Katherine Holubitsky (Orca)
Marking Time and *Confusion*, Elizabeth Jane Howard (Pan MacMillan)
The Magician's Nephew, C. S. Lewis (HarperCollins)
The Names They Gave Us, Emery Lloyd (Bloomsbury)
On Eagles' Wings and *Patterns in the Sand*, Sue Mayfield (Lion)
A Monster Calls by Patrick Ness (Walker Books)
Paper Aeroplanes, Dawn O'Porter (Hot Key Books)
Grief is the Thing with Feathers, Max Porter (Faber & Faber)
The Wild Other, Clover Stroud (Hodder)
Wipe Out, Mimi Thebo (HarperCollins)
How not to be a Boy, Robert Webb (Canongate)

Losing a sibling:
My Sister Lives on the Mantelpiece, Annabel Pitcher (Hatchette)
The Catcher in the Rye, J. D. Salinger (Penguin)
The Life and Death of Charlie St Cloud, Ben Sherwood (Pan MacMillan)

The Last Act of Love, Cathy Rentzenbrink (Pan MacMillan)
Where the Past Begins, Amy Tan (HarperCollins) – also the loss of a father

Losing a friend/boyfriend/girlfriend

Vicky Angel, Jacqueline Wilson (Random House)
The Fault in Our Stars, John Green (Penguin)
Goodbye Days, Jeff Zentner (Anderson Press)

Non-fiction

Academic studies

Healing Children's Grief, Grace Hyslop Christ (Oxford University Press)
Living with Grief after Sudden Loss, edited by Kenneth J. Doka (Routledge)
Supporting Traumatised Children and Teenagers, Atle Dyregrov (Jessica Kingsley)
An Intimate Loneliness: Supporting Bereaved Parents and Siblings, Gordon Riches and Pam Dawson (Open University Press)

Where is God?

Everything Happens for a Reason and Other Lies I've Loved, Kate Bowler (SPCK)
Is God to Blame? Greg Boyd (IVP)
A Brief History of Heaven, Alister McGrath (John Wiley and Sons)
Surprised by Hope, Tom Wright (SPCK)

Mental health support

The Man Who Couldn't Stop, David Adam (Pan MacMillan) – helpful for health anxiety & OCD
Motherless Daughters, Hope Edelman (Lifelong Books)

Grieving a Suicide, Albert Y. Hsu (IVP)

Grief Works: Stories of Life, Death and Surviving, Juliet Samuel (Penguin)

Tackling Health Anxiety: A CBT Handbook, Helen Tyrer (RCPsych Publications)

Medicine

Being Mortal: Illness, Medicine, and What Matters in the End, Atul Gawande (Profile Books)

Dying Well, John Wyatt (IVP)

Sources of help

These charities all offer a range of phone, email and live-chat help-lines that you can contact for support

At A Loss is a Christian charity, but it offers to support to anyone who has been bereaved **www.ataloss.org/projects/grab-life**

Brake is a road safety charity that offers a huge amount of information and support for families **www.brake.org.uk**

Child Bereavement UK offers specific support to young people including a collection of personal stories and support groups for people aged 11 to 25 **www.childbereavementuk.org/young-people**

Grief Encounter offers support to young people, including free e-counselling over Skype for people aged 14 or over **www.griefencounter.org.uk**

Hope Again is the youth website of Cruse Bereavement Care, with a focus on bringing together the stories of young people **www.hopeagain.org.uk**

The National Association for Children of Alcoholics (NACOA) offers excellent advice for young people affected by a parent's drinking, including information on how to stay safe **www.nacoa.org.uk**

Winston's Wish, a charity that supports bereaved children and young people, has a special website for young people **https://help2makesense.org**

Need to talk urgently?

If you ever feel that you are in crisis, or might hurt yourself, it's so important that you speak to someone. Although the helplines listed above are open for a limited number of hours, there are some that you can call at any time of day or night, seven days a week. All of those listed below are free:

The Samaritans 116 123

Childline 0800 111 (Also available is a 1-2-1 Counsellor Chat: **https://childline.org.uk/get-support/1-2-1-counsellor-chat**)

The **YoungMinds** Crisis Messenger offers a text service specifically for people aged 25 and under, at 85258

WE HAVE A VISION OF A WORLD IN WHICH EVERYONE IS TRANSFORMED BY CHRISTIAN KNOWLEDGE

As well as being an award-winning publisher, SPCK is the oldest Anglican mission agency in the world.

Our mission is to lead the way in creating books and resources that help everyone to make sense of faith.

Will you partner with us to put good books into the hands of prisoners and great assemblies in front of schoolchildren and to reach out to people who have not yet been touched by the Christian faith?

To donate, please visit <www.spckpublishing.co.uk/donate> or call our friendly fundraising team on 020 7592 3900.